# Competitive SME

DI051220

# Competitive SME

Building competitive advantage through marketing excellence for small to medium sized enterprises

David James Hood

KoganPage

LONDON  PHILADELPHIA  NEW DELHI

First published in Great Britain and the United States in 2013 by Kogan Page Limited

| | | |
|---|---|---|
| 120 Pentonville Road | 1518 Walnut Street, Suite 1100 | 4737/23 Ansari Road |
| London N1 9JN | Philadelphia PA 19102 | Daryaganj |
| United Kingdom | USA | New Delhi 110002 |
| www.koganpage.com | | India |

© David James Hood, 2013

The right of David James Hood to be identified as the author of this work has been asserted by him in accordance with the Copyright, Designs and Patents Act 1988.

ISBN      978 0 7494 6850 7
E-ISBN   978 0 7494 6851 4

**British Library Cataloguing-in-Publication Data**

A CIP record for this book is available from the British Library.

**Library of Congress Cataloging-in-Publication Data**

Hood, David J.
    Competitive SME : building competitive advantage through marketing excellence for small to medium sized enterprises / David Hood.
        p. cm.
    Includes index.
    ISBN 978-0-7494-6850-7 – ISBN 978-0-7494-6851-4    1. Small business marketing.    I. Title.
    HF5415.13.H667 2013
    658.8–dc23

                                                                                                2012032991

Typeset by Graphicraft Limited, Hong Kong
Printed and bound in India by Replika Press Pvt Ltd

## Dedication

*To my soulmate Eleanor,* mo leannan sìth,
*who invigorates my existence with constant
inspiration and encouragement and who along
with my delightful daughters Laura and Jennifer give
me a sense of privilege and purpose; my lovingly
remembered mother Irene for encouraging me to always
ask questions; and good friends, family and colleagues
who ensure my feet are kept firmly on the ground
by offering their welcome and invigorating probity.*

# CONTENTS

# LIST OF FIGURES
# AND TABLES

## Figures

# Tables

# ACKNOWLEDGEMENTS

Thanks go to my friend and associate Professor Umit Bititci and colleagues on the European Union backed *futureSME*™ project Dr Aylin Ates and Dr Catherine Maguire; Jim Mather for his thoughtful foreword to the book and ongoing stimulus, Brian Canavan of Aperture for his growing contributions to SME marketing within the Competitive SME initiative community and work on the proposition accelerator tool; and of course, to small and medium-sized enterprises – without which there would be no *large* enterprises, a severe lack of 'big ideas' and indeed no commerce whatsoever on planet earth.

My thanks also extend to the Microsoft Dynamics and Microsoft SMB Europe teams for supporting this book and to Global Marketing Network's founder and CEO Darrell Kofkin and its Chair, Ian Derbyshire, for 'sharing the vision' to actively enhance marketing practice, and to Matt Smith, Head Publisher at Kogan Page, for broadening the scope and opportunity for our shared ambitions.

# FOREWORD

This is a book for the busy manager in small to medium-sized enterprises. Its main thrust is to make the case for SMEs adopting an outside-to-inside understanding of their market and customers rather than the opposite company-centric perspective. Not only does the book spell out the advantages of this approach but it also shows the reader how to achieve that end.

In doing so, David Hood covers some basic marketing themes relating to competitiveness and makes a general case for marketing. This is appropriate, for most of us have a sketchy understanding of the subject and many of us do not get involved in marketing to the extent that we could and should do.

David does this really well and establishes that marketing is not creative spin; that in fact it is vital both externally and internally to bring clarity to the mission – and crucially that it is easier and more affordable than we generally assume. He also helps us develop a real understanding of the outside-to-inside journey, which he does by 'de-layering' the entire proposition rather than the usual 'value-add' addition of layers.

In doing this, he gives SMEs a gentle nudge towards only considering offerings to be 'added-value' when customers agree with that status and genuinely see and appreciate that value.

Aligned with that he has tackled the cost-plus and cost-centric approach to pricing and product development, not only to encourage SMEs to use another means to create and price 'value propositions' but indeed to show that the cost-based approach leads to inadvertent commoditization and a devaluing of the goods and services being delivered.

In addition, he offers us some real insights – such as the tendencies for many SMEs to:

- Miss the opportunity to link marketing and market awareness to develop even more valuable and profitable propositions that would appeal to existing and new customers.

- Be too comfortable with the core product, and much less happy with development of the wider augmented proposition that could benefit customers, foster word-of-mouth marketing and produce additional revenues.

- See marketing as a cost, not an investment; making the mistake of categorizing it as a series of promotional gimmicks rather than a tight feedback mechanism that gains more sales and improves the product and services.

- Fail to see that markets, groups of prospects, customers and consumers are now self-organizing and re-writing the business landscape; they are more knowledgeable; and with the advent of data protection, changing attitudes to corporate conduct and new technologies and social media, they are increasingly in control.

- Fail to understand that a move from a product focus to a market focus prevents them achieving a far better balance between invention and market-based innovation.

- Fail to see that they and other SMEs are actually better placed than large corporations to deliver better service and have greater understanding of the customer by being more agile and not simply more creative. In other words, they can get closer to their customer and can be more appreciated.

- Fail to resist the temptation to improve everywhere; or to see that the *key* problem for SMEs is stress – on its owners and managers – and it is biological rather than merely the material. They therefore need to do *less* accordingly; so to be able to focus on improvements only where they will result in enhanced and more competitive propositions not only makes obvious sense, but reduces that core problem of SME-stress. (Likewise being able to focus on the customers and prospects with large core challenges and opportunities makes a lot of sense and reduces stress further.)

- Fail to see that everyone is involved in marketing; all the SME's people and the agents or others further down the SMEs supply chain.

- Fail to see that every SME has a great story to tell; they also have the capability to create new stories based on their understanding of the market and their own context within the market (rather than the all too prevalent 'look what we have done' PR stories that feature in business media articles).

- Fail to fully capitalize on the fact that SMEs have more to gain by managing a credible projection of trustworthiness than larger companies.

- Fail to move from the principle of 'make to stock' to 'make to order' – or in other words, make what the market wants rather than what we wish to sell – and a corresponding change to better metrics. Market share is no longer sufficient as a measurement; what is needed is the SME's own specific definition of 'its market', simply defined as a reasonable level of engagement with sufficient customers with sufficiently large problems or opportunities that the SME can help them with; and a marked move from 'purchasing benefits' (for example that are reflected in the wrongful assumption that lower price is somehow more value to the market) to operational benefits (decidedly helping make the customers more money or making their lives better). Also addressed is the old chestnut that is the focus on attracting new custom over delivering better and more often to existing customers.

In addition, the book confirms what most people have known for some time that good word of mouth is the major metric, or at least the major objective to help make money.

What was needed – and this book provides – is a means to measure, influence and manage it. Indeed, it looks at customer relationship management (CRM) through this prism and readdresses CRM as a process that seeks to better measure what we deliver rather than just one-way contact with the market. CRM = a sense and respond process; not just to manage our 'telling, yelling and selling' to it. Word of mouth also leads to greater 'pull' rather than costly 'push' in terms of locus for activities, improved ROI for the SME in marketing and product development, and increasing the SME's power in the market.

The book also proves that branding considerations can be easily applied to the SME and that branding is not just a large corporation issue; likewise some powerful, simple but not simplistic means can be used to assess what the market thinks, how it positions the SME, its proposition and the competition in the market; and that, even occasionally managed, can add a lot to the proposition and its positioning in the mind of those they would wish to influence.

In short, this is a book for those SMEs that want to be profitable and adaptive, successful and resilient and want to enjoy the process and to leave a positive legacy.

*Jim Mather, past Minister for Enterprise,*
*The Scottish Government*

# Introduction

> *Business has two – and only two – functions: marketing and innovation.* **PETER F DRUCKER**

## Why you should read this book

Let us get things very clear from the outset; this book is about *maintaining and improving revenue*. It is specifically created to meet the needs of the small to medium-sized enterprise (SME) throughout Europe and beyond, and it is clearly presented in a no-nonsense, practical format. You can read the whole book, or scan for a quick resolution to your immediate challenges or to help seize new opportunities. The book complements the futureSME™ initiative in helping SMEs attain adaptive competitive capabilities.

## How to use this book and what you will get from it

This book is specifically constructed for you, the SME owner, director, manager or executive, to get the most out of it. Each chapter outlines *a) what needs to change, b) what that change would result in and c) how to change.*

*Crucial and significant aspects and items for the SME are highlighted using this icon:*

You are given the opportunity throughout the book to check your own competitiveness in the market and your own product and proposition's uniqueness and potency; improving that proposition and whilst doing so, improving your own personal skills to create opportunities to maintain and improve revenue.

# A straightforward seven-stage path to competitiveness through enhanced marketing

Figure 1.1 is a summary of the path recommended in this book; a fuller map is contained in the final chapter, but this is offered now to show the process as a simple seven-stage series of actions. The individual components are explained later in the book.

The book's structure means you can dip into relevant sections at your leisure, *but it is recommended that you read it as a whole* to get the most for your organization; to make a real step forward in working towards sustainable, indelible competitive advantage. You will see later that the thrust of this book will demonstrate the 'competitive marketing triangle' that guides you to establish:

- revenue now;
- revenue soon;
- revenue in the near future.

# Practical book and tools

Explaining the necessary ingredients for success in each chapter is essential to set the background for the reader, before moving on rapidly to identify what changes are needed to improve competitiveness and revenue generation capabilities and offer a definitive way forward, actually covering the 'HOW'. There are a number of practical, powerful real-world SME marketing and competitiveness tools throughout this book: and I have used two ways to quickly assess where you currently are: a Likert-scale marketing checklist at the outset and a 'competitiveness radar map graph' (The Competitive Marketing Triangle) at the end that illustrate the key elements to success so you can readily plot them as you set about improving your 'edge' and resulting revenue.

*In addition to summary tables and illustrations at the end of the chapters, the tools are also listed in the table within Chapter 8 and in the concluding overall map in Chapter 12 to help you to use them quickly in order and as necessary.* There are also, for those of you who wish it, links to further reading, tools and knowledge to ensure that, whatever improvements you make, they are made as effectively as possible and long lasting. *The 'path' in Figure 1.1 shows how you can rapidly use the tools in an uncomplicated, methodical and sequenced manner.*

**FIGURE 1.1**   Competitive SME seven-stage path

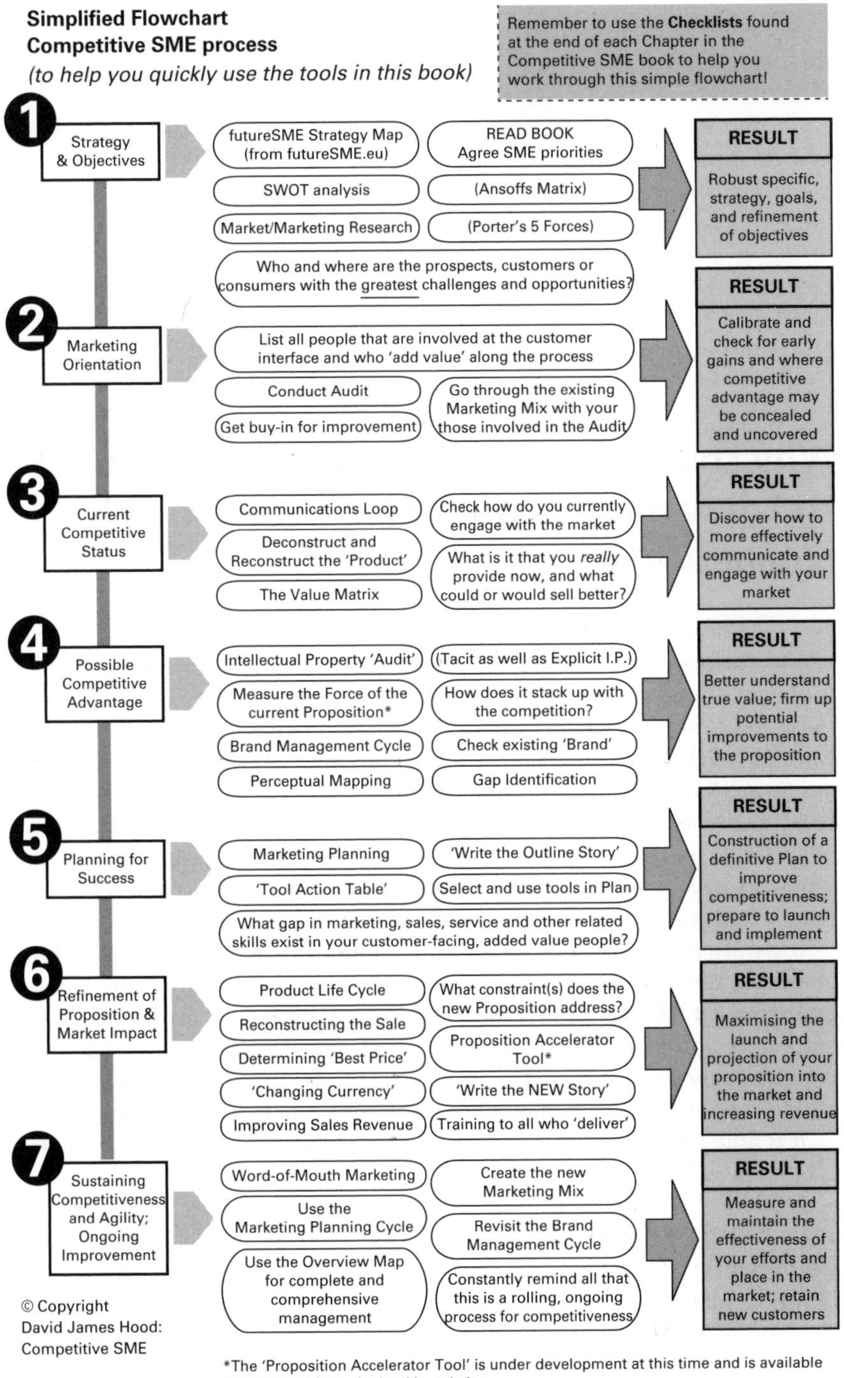

**Simplified Flowchart**
**Competitive SME process**
*(to help you quickly use the tools in this book)*

Remember to use the **Checklists** found at the end of each Chapter in the Competitive SME book to help you work through this simple flowchart!

**1 Strategy & Objectives**
- futureSME Strategy Map (from futureSME.eu)
- READ BOOK Agree SME priorities
- SWOT analysis
- (Ansoffs Matrix)
- Market/Marketing Research
- (Porter's 5 Forces)
- Who and where are the prospects, customers or consumers with the greatest challenges and opportunities?

**RESULT** Robust specific, strategy, goals, and refinement of objectives

**2 Marketing Orientation**
- List all people that are involved at the customer interface and who 'add value' along the process
- Conduct Audit
- Go through the existing Marketing Mix with your those involved in the Audit
- Get buy-in for improvement

**RESULT** Calibrate and check for early gains and where competitive advantage may be concealed and uncovered

**3 Current Competitive Status**
- Communications Loop
- Check how do you currently engage with the market
- Deconstruct and Reconstruct the 'Product'
- What is it that you *really* provide now, and what could or would sell better?
- The Value Matrix

**RESULT** Discover how to more effectively communicate and engage with your market

**4 Possible Competitive Advantage**
- Intellectual Property 'Audit'
- (Tacit as well as Explicit I.P.)
- Measure the Force of the current Proposition*
- How does it stack up with the competition?
- Brand Management Cycle
- Check existing 'Brand'
- Perceptual Mapping
- Gap Identification

**RESULT** Better understand true value; firm up potential improvements to the proposition

**5 Planning for Success**
- Marketing Planning
- 'Write the Outline Story'
- 'Tool Action Table'
- Select and use tools in Plan
- What gap in marketing, sales, service and other related skills exist in your customer-facing, added value people?

**RESULT** Construction of a definitive Plan to improve competitiveness; prepare to launch and implement

**6 Refinement of Proposition & Market Impact**
- Product Life Cycle
- What constraint(s) does the new Proposition address?
- Reconstructing the Sale
- Proposition Accelerator Tool*
- Determining 'Best Price'
- 'Changing Currency'
- 'Write the NEW Story'
- Improving Sales Revenue
- Training to all who 'deliver'

**RESULT** Maximising the launch and projection of your proposition into the market and increasing revenue

**7 Sustaining Competitiveness and Agility; Ongoing Improvement**
- Word-of-Mouth Marketing
- Create the new Marketing Mix
- Use the Marketing Planning Cycle
- Revisit the Brand Management Cycle
- Use the Overview Map for complete and comprehensive management
- Constantly remind all that this is a rolling, ongoing process for competitiveness

**RESULT** Measure and maintain the effectiveness of your efforts and place in the market; retain new customers

© Copyright
David James Hood:
Competitive SME

*The 'Proposition Accelerator Tool' is under development at this time and is available downloaded from the book's website

## Clear definitions and direction for the SME

I have tried to keep away from jargon – especially unnecessary jargon – in this book, but unfortunately, we do need to use some of the language of business and so I have included my own definitions as they apply to this book and in helping your efforts to improve your competitive advantage and revenue generating capabilities.

Brevity is the keyword with this book; I have kept things to the bare minimum so that you, the SME owner, manager, or executive with a need to 'bring in the money', can use it quickly and effectively. I do however, encourage you to go further and look at how these 'quick wins' can be further developed into something more durable and to help you to sustain your competitive capabilities.

## Why should I care about marketing? I want to know more about being exceptionally competitive!

The quotation from Drucker at the start of this chapter says it all. The SME has to focus on both its capabilities to technically innovate, to efficiently produce for and service its market, and constantly improve that capability; but it has to do so with more than just a passing affirmation and validation from its market. *Too many good intentions, new inventions, concepts, products, modified propositions and 'innovations' have been thwarted by the harsh reality of the market.* Being 'innovative' for the sake of it, to improve one's own, or the company's own productivity and inventiveness is one thing; to have a product and full proposition that is most attractive and critical and willingly purchased by the market may be quite another.

If we attempt to become, or sustain, an innovative organization without involving the market we are seriously myopic. Eventually every action, improvement, challenge, or other worthy activity has to involve sales and marketing and hence the market; *but not just towards the end of the product development process.* The market has to be involved at the start, the middle and at the end. And at all times in-between, before and after.

*It is now time to let those important marketing and competitive processes take the lead!*

DON'T PUT THIS BOOK DOWN SIMPLY BECAUSE YOU SEE THE WORD 'MARKETING' IN IT... the majority of concerns for SMEs discovered by the futureSME™ project across Europe are MARKETING ISSUES... (and other top issues are influenced by marketing too)...

... SO PLEASE READ ON!

**TABLE 1.1**  futureSME™ project and marketing issues

| futureSME project: challenges identified | Marketing issues related to those challenges |
|---|---|
| Sales and marketing **(the #1 issue!)** | Overall improvement and alignment between both activities, *to make more money*; the need for a real and consistent presence in the market |
| Strategy | The need to have a clear idea where we are going, why and how; we need to be *different* |
| Customer interaction / management | How do we manage relationships with the market and use 'CRM'? |
| Performance management | What should be measured and where should we invest, that actually helps us generate more revenue? |
| Communication | How can we maximize our dialogue with the market and make a greater impact in it? |
| Culture | Can we really make ourselves 'customer-centric' or 'market oriented'? Why and how? |
| Leadership | How do we rally our people to create and sustain something truly remarkable and how can I personally make this happen? |
| Production efficiency | How can we ensure that we always make things that will sell more easily? |
| Value proposition | We need to fight increasing competitiveness in the marketplace; what should we offer? |
| Management system | We need a an overriding system that guides and paces our SME to make money |
| Skills, training and collaboration | Focus only on the improvements, resources and skills that will result in making money |
| Market scanning | Definition of markets, what market should we be in and how can we influence it |
| New Product and Service Development | Align with market need, offer the best propositions and get the best price for them |
| New Product and Service Introduction | How can we get the 'biggest bang' in the market and establish our position within it? |

# Marketing: what it is; and just as important, what it is not

Everyone has his or her own interpretation of what marketing is. Surprisingly sometimes, it is not even seen as part of the innovative or competitive process at all. Indeed, marketing is often left out of strategy and the plans to make money for the organization. Left out, until the end of the process, as an afterthought. How has that happened? Well, let us look briefly at some of the popular misconceptions about marketing, its definitions and interpretations that, if addressed, can help us grasp and exploit it so that we may use marketing to improve our competitiveness and revenue generation capabilities.

**FIGURE 1.2**    Note!

It really is necessary at this point to recap on what marketing is if you plan to make some money from improving it, as it is continually thought to be anything to do with advertising, with a bit of promotions and logos 'thrown in' to force and coerce people to buy.

However, let us remember that marketing started *IN THE MARKET*. That thriving, wonderful and colourful hub of complete human interaction and fundamental commerce where human beings have shared and exchanged things of value for centuries.

*That is what marketing was, and what it should continue to be.*

Organizations, companies, sales, distribution channels and all sorts of commercial activities ignore this and business people forget this simple fact. Indeed, as organizations and commerce become more complex and activities and roles more specialized, exclusive and set apart from the other activities and roles in the organization, the fundamental practice of two-way human communication with the market has become all but lost. Strikingly, larger organizations are the worst offenders and are poorer 'marketers' than many SMEs.

## What marketing is NOT

Marketing is NOT just 'creative advertising', with a bit of promotional activity and selling thrown in. It is not just about making up stories to trick and cajole an unwilling and uninterested market. It is not simply 'telling, yelling and selling'. It is seen by many, including experienced and wise business people, as nothing more than one-way, unwarranted, unwanted and interruptive promotional activities.

## What marketing ACTUALLY IS

It is a virtuous set of policies, principles and processes that ensure that: a) we make what the market actually needs and wants, and b) will make us more profitable by properly engaging with the market. It is honest, virtuous and ensures that the organization generates real value; it is a means of holding multiple conversations and meaningful engagement with all of your so-called 'stakeholders' to the benefit and profit of all.

*Marketing is arguably the creation and exchange of any-thing of value that is made possible by eloquent human ingenuity and interaction.*

Marketing therefore encompasses all points where value is created and exchanged, and includes *all processes* by which the organization realizes its core revenue generating objectives.

*This book outlines the necessary change to what we describe and perform under the term and process of 'competitiveness in the market', to make our propositions truly and substantively more attractive and to reduce or eliminate market resistance to sales.*

So read on...!

# A short and essential history

**FIGURE 1.3**   The dimensions of marketing

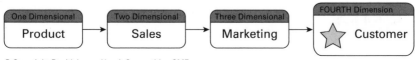

© Copyright David James Hood: Competitive SME

Business, as it relates to its 'front end' commercial operations, is said to have gone through about three (and now four) major historic and cultural phases – evolutions or new dimensions, if you like.

The first was a *product focus* where, due to the limited number of manu-facturing producers and suppliers for the buyer to consider, the manufactur-ers just had to provide a product. They did not need to do much with it other than make it available. This situation changed with the onset of greater competition in the market, with a correspondingly greater variety of prod-uct and service options and sources or places to buy.

The next metamorphosis for commerce gave us the *sales focus*. This meant that manufacturing organizations, together with their ever more

numerous and complex supply chains, moved to developing ways to crea-
tively and forcibly enhance their proposition in the eyes of the market.
Differences were established and communicated more and more effectively,
using greater and more diverse promotional methods and means to 'get to
the customer or consumer'. These two phases of business and commerce
could be said to be primarily transactional; a wholly insufficient situation
and attitude, yet one born of its time. Modern times though, required a more
mature and modern approach. In comes the *third focus – marketing –* that
was to be the panacea; instead of making what we make then selling it to
anyone that would listen (or could be coerced into buying), marketing was
meant to be the 'top and tail' of the development of markets and products
so that the organization could provide the right product, for the right market, in the right way; actually aligning product development and delivery
and 'making to need'. A '3D' approach as it were; this time it was not to be
a focus merely on the transaction, but a focus on satisfying the real and
underlying need that would in turn make the customer have a greater want
for the product or service.

*We are now moving to the fourth focus or era, one
of 'CUSTOMER FOCUS' or 'REVERSE CUSTOMER
CONVERGENCE' – whether the customers are in consumer or business-to-business markets, they are in charge
now, and coming together to communicate and compare in the way
that they wish to!* This is the new collaborative, co-created and almost self-
organized re-embodiment of business. We cannot ignore it and we need to
warmly embrace it.

'Marketing is arguably the creation and exchange of
anything of value.'

This all means that your 'downstream' customer or end-user consumer – the
individual organizations and customers further down your supply chain –
are becoming more knowledgeable and empowered, and this affects all
of the chain and, in particular for you, it directly affects your immediate
customer. Your supply chain now needs, just as much as you do, to be more
competitive than ever before. You and your downstream customer both
need to 'harness the unharnessable' – the empowered end-customer or
consumer that is unashamedly and increasingly self-organizing their own
product exploration and buying environment.

Bill Gates stated 'If the 1980s were about quality and the 1990s about re-engineering, then the 2000s will be about velocity.' I think that the 2010s is about INTIMACY and ENGAGEMENT... linked to the rise of the customer and the consumer. As such, we urgently need to look at advancing our sense and respond systems to align with these new self-creating markets and CO-CREATE with our customers and consumers. (We could put data inputs from these channels directly into our new product and service development programmes right now if we chose to do so!)

These four periods or progressions have evolved successively over the entire 20th century and now into the 21st. Each improved somewhat on the previous. HOWEVER, our organizations are still regrettably 'unevolved' when it comes to matching the actual need of the customer or consumer with our resources and skills to invent and make. This is reflected in the difficulties that most SMEs have in creating an authentic and commanding advantage and then remaining competitive thereafter.

*We are stuck, underperforming, in the 3rd era...*

Why should this be so? Why are we underperforming?

The demands of the market rarely completely match the demands and the capabilities of the business. We still have a focus on the basic premise of making what we want to make and thrashing the market into giving in to our promotions and taking our products and services. What is set out in this book is a means to use traditional marketing tools along with new practical, timely and wholly implementable modern ideas that can really make your SME thrive and evolve to 'exploit the fourth dimension'.

##  Using the book in conjunction with the futureSME initiative

This book has been produced in association with the European Union initiative of the same name – futureSME™. The format complements and parallels the thrust of that initiative; it can be used to best effect when coupled with the diagnostic report and strategy map found within the futureSME™ website and complements these resources and methods by focusing on three competitive manifestations for the SME: Strategy, Resilience and Adaptability:

- *Strategy:*
  (focus on the levers of creating the greatest amount of revenue and planning for it; better alignment of the market with the organization and vice versa).

- *Adaptability:*
  (to *remain* competitive and display agility based on the structure of sensing and serving the market and the accumulation of real insights and intelligence of the market and its needs).

● *Resilience:*
(to be sufficiently competitive and keep revenue coming in and constant).

Competitive SME is, for the purposes of the initiative and in particular this book, about crafting an SME that never ceases to be agile in terms of its ability to sense and respond with competitive propositions, at the forefront of its market.

I have consciously structured and written this book so that it does the following for the SME and the owner or manager:

● *encompasses and updates the marketing basics you need to help create competitive advantage in the market;*

● *focuses on the single best route to developing an authentic unique selling proposition (USP);*

● *gives you the means for sustaining that advantage.*

**FIGURE 1.4** Summary of the essentials from this chapter

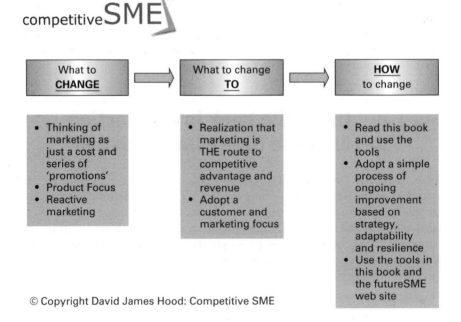

competitive SME™

| What to CHANGE | What to change TO | HOW to change |
|---|---|---|
| • Thinking of marketing as just a cost and series of 'promotions'<br>• Product Focus<br>• Reactive marketing | • Realization that marketing is THE route to competitive advantage and revenue<br>• Adopt a customer and marketing focus | • Read this book and use the tools<br>• Adopt a simple process of ongoing improvement based on strategy, adaptability and resilience<br>• Use the tools in this book and the futureSME web site |

© Copyright David James Hood: Competitive SME

*Innovation is the process of turning ideas into manufacturable and marketable form.* **WATTS HUMPHREY**

# The reality

## Addressing stress for the SME owner, manager or executive

*"Stress is an ignorant state. It believes that everything is an emergency.* NATALIE GOLDBERG

## Achieving a sound sleep at night...

In creating this book for the SME, I have consciously endeavoured not only to spell out what the SME can do to enhance its competitiveness through grasping the opportunities existing in 'getting marketing right', but I also reflected on the truism that the SME owner, manager and executive *suffers greatly*.

You constantly suffer daily as you have to make difficult decisions, always seem to have limited or insufficient resources, and where wrong decisions, investments and actions can prove fatal for the business. It goes without saying that if the SME's key people – including you – are constantly unhappy with that stress, then the organization will not be as effective.

We all suffer personally from the challenges of business from time to time, and people within SMEs arguably suffer more than those within larger organizations. Sometimes there is no let-up from difficulties, with continual day-to-day fire-fighting and one new problem replacing another. As individual people in small organizations, we tend to have a lot of weight on our shoulders; we invariably have more than one role to play in our organization, we have many things to do and when the buck stops, it stops right at our door or desk. Compounding this problem of course, is that *we are expected and told to embrace big company ideas and initiatives*, everywhere, always. More, more, more. One initiative, change or new thing to do after another. On and on and on.

What I find frustrating and infuriating is that the do-gooders, the 'improvement chattering classes', all tell those of us who own or manage SMEs that we should try this latest initiative or that, and suggest to us that some wonderful initiative or change has been good for big corporations so it must be something we should aspire to emulate.

Well, this simply doesn't help; SMEs' problems differ greatly and are of a different magnitude and express themselves differently than they do in large corporations with their seemingly infinite resources, greater clout, wider choice of markets, and their apparent abilities to absorb and address problems. In addition, of course, large companies can more or less try anything, any new improvement option – but we SMEs cannot afford that luxury or risk. Therefore, there really is only one option...

*So, what is proposed here is for you, the SME manager or owner, to actually DO LESS when it comes to change and improvement.*

Let the large corporations spend and lose a lot of money and time on innovating everywhere, following each whim and whimsy that the chattering classes (and marketing agencies and technology companies) tell them is best for them. What we have in this book and at the heart of the Competitive SME project is a focus; we do not encourage you to 'innovate everywhere', and therefore help the SME concentrate on where finite areas of competitiveness may lie and short-listing where any improvements ought to be made.

The opening remark in this chapter from Natalie Goldberg rings true with those of us who have to manage or own an SME; we simply have too many things to do. Too much pressure coming from too many sources. Everything to do with working in an SME is considered an emergency or priority, likewise every opportunity or challenge is given equal status. *Therefore, what is proposed here is actually to do LESS, but that does mean we need to know what to do and what not to do.* Therein dwells the answer and the opportunity: let us make the few, finite, changes and concentrate only where we will make the most returns – ie gain the highest return on investment of our very limited time, money and resources.

 That is why I am confident that we can address the #1 *issue for the SME – unwanted and unhealthy stress on its key people –* that severely affects management attention, decision-making and the ability to focus.

*Every single chapter in this book is dedicated to reducing stress on you, your company and its people.*

... Now read on!

# The reality for SMEs and turning things to your advantage

So, we all have major personal stresses, and those are compounded by the pressure to adopt the big ideas and latest fad and consider tales of 'big company x did this and that is why they became better.' We wrongly think we can reduce stress and better our business lives by constantly following the latest new fad. But this of course ADDS to our stress!

In seeking to turn things to our advantage as an SME, we should consider WHY we are different from larger corporations, and what that actually means to us in helping improve our competitiveness and ability to generate revenue. We can see very quickly why our view of the world from our SME is just as valid; it is neither wrong nor less evolved than the view of big companies, it is merely different. Different from large corporate concepts and so-called 'solutions'.

*'Want to know the big secret to SME success over larger companies? Larger companies just don't care about their customers – but **you do. Simple!**'*

Could we ignore the fad or the latest guru-inspired 'business re-engineering' theory and focus on only finite and realistic changes that can and should be applied to an SME? *I think that we must.* We have to focus only on 'certainties'; and even if there are precious few certainties in our SME world, there are FAR too many initiatives and ideas to improve that are certainly never going to result in a certain return. Table 2.1 outlines just some of those differences between the large corporation and the SME.

Table 2.1 lists only some of the differences between large companies and SMEs. The SME's reality is somewhat different from the larger corporate organization; something that you and I know and something that the 'chattering classes' that advise the SME tend to forget. What could be construed as a weakness – the SMEs inability to do a whole spread of activities, initiatives and trial-and-error – is perhaps its greatest strength; but only if we cut down on all those so-called initiatives and changes that we could do in preference for those that we should do. And stop playing the big corporate game.

**TABLE 2.1**  Big companies and SMEs

| Big Company Concepts | SME *Realities* |
|---|---|
| They tend to be organized, better resourced and maintain resources and foresight for innovation and improvement | Ad-hoc tactical improvements are made mainly when provoked into making change and when resources allow |
| Innovate constantly and try new things everywhere and anywhere we can | Innovate only where we can ensure we make money and can afford to invest (or lose) it |
| A big spread of risks, investments and activities means that the company will be more likely to succeed | We need to stick to making real changes to our customer or consumers well-being; not spreading risk, but focusing |
| They can play the long game; investing and developing products for the future and can afford to lose frequently and gamble | We need to reduce our product ranges, adapt quickly and cannot afford long term developments as markets change too rapidly |
| Throw money at promoting their products everywhere and try each and every new channel, technology, by whatever means | Focus our marketing and communications efforts and new technologies to critical channels that result in engagement |
| Create a wide range of propositions so that everyone that could be their customer, should be | Chose carefully which customer has the biggest problem that we can fix and focus on it |
| Make what they want to make, at the margins they wish, and sell them to a lot of markets in many different ways | Make what the market needs, now, to ensure we can make the most money possible whilst our advantage lasts |
| The main 'customers' are really the shareholders and 'the city' who seize money **from** the organization | The main customers are those who pay money **to** the organization |
| **They encourage and nurture complexity** | **We favour and desire *simplicity*** |

*You don't actually have to change everything and everywhere to improve value and profit*

This seems pretty reasonable to suggest doesn't it? It may sound compelling even? Your intuition would surely suggest that it is best for an organization to only change in certain ways and in certain places. This results in trimming down money and resources invested in changing many of your processes, proposition options or company 'improvements'; *focusing your investments and resources on things that will make you money*, AND by definition, saving you from wasting money and resources on activities and propositions that simply will not sustain or improve revenue. To know precisely, what NOT to do, is arguably as important as knowing precisely where to focus your efforts and hard-earned money on improvements.

# Reducing personal stress

If we subscribe to the idea that we can reduce stress by accepting that we are best to do only a few, distinct changes and activities that get us 'the biggest bang for our buck', then we can truly liberate ourselves as professional business people. Stress is caused by 'being out or control'; whether it is real or perceived, stress is corrosive and unlike many facets to our lives is cumulative, doesn't always make sense, and affects our individual and corporate abilities.

This book will have failed if it does not help you address this #1 problem for small to medium-sized business people; we need to increase our prowess, so *we need to know what decisions have to be taken now* to reduce stress and put in place better processes and measurements that will result in stress becoming a thing of the past. We can start that process by determining 'who is responsible for what' when it comes to keeping the organization 'healthy' and how others within it can help make clearer decisions now that affect the future for the better, and additionally determine what new changes need to be make now to make that improvement to our personal health indelible and long-lasting.

Lead not in creativity, but in competitiveness in the organization and delegate day-to-day sales and marketing to others. This will involve some investment, in time as well as money, but a day spent on competitiveness as outlined in this book is worth many more spent simply fire-fighting and tactically scraping the odd campaign and promotional activities together.

If you can lead through focusing on competitiveness, creativity will follow or at least be induced in the right way and as an answer to a real problem and opportunity for the organization. Creativity for its own sake is not that clever – remember the Sinclair C5! So how do we achieve this? How can I help you sleep continuously through the night without wakening in the middle of the night worrying about the next day-to-day fire-fight or where the next buck, euro or pound is coming from, etc etc?

# Changing 'cannot' to 'can'

In realizing that 'SME stress' results in large part from the peculiarities of running an SME, we see that 'big company' initiatives are not relevant, as we become very close to our market and its needs. If you can prioritize by the needs and constraints of your market you lessen risk, reducing the load on you, your people and your organization. Having a focus means that not only do you only do what you should or need to be doing; importantly you discard other options, changes, initiatives, ideas etc that you should not do, as they are simply clouding your mind and getting in the way of success.

Less *can* be more.

Key *constraints* are the key to profits.

Management attention is a key constraint on *us*, so reduce that burden!

Leverage constraints and key 'marketing mix' elements.

Alignment with the market.

Sense and respond.

Kill the vacuum.

**FIGURE 2.1**    Summary of the essentials from this chapter

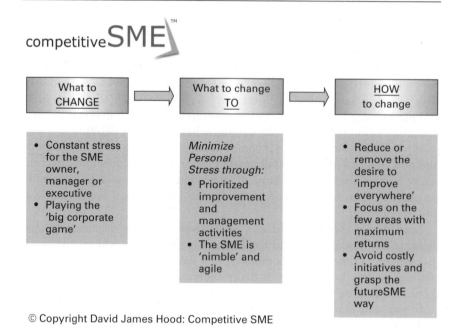

© Copyright David James Hood: Competitive SME

**FIGURE 2.2**   Chapter 2 summary action table

| ☑ | CHAPTER 2 Summary Action Table |
|---|---|
| ☐ | Take steps to prioritise your options, changes and improvements to reduce stress |
| ☐ | Discount 'big company' ideas and narrow down to what works for an SME |
| ☐ | Start to look at and choose customers and prospects who have the larger problems and opportunities |

© Copyright David James Hood: Competitive SME

Are you thinking 'can I really do any of this?' *Great. Read on...*

*The greatest weapon against stress is our ability to choose one thought over another.*

**WILLIAM JAMES**

# Competitiveness and the SME

## We want it; but how do we get it?

> *We are surrounded by engineers' follies: too many technical solutions still looking for problems to solve.* **DAVID TANSLE**

## Forget 'Pareto's principle'?

When it comes to competitiveness, and for that matter improving your organization's ability to deliver products and make money, it isn't 20 per cent of issues, processes, problems etc that are causing 80 per cent of your challenges or unrealized opportunities – it is actually only a few percent. VERY few problems are actually causing your major challenges in business. *Likewise, only a few changes to your organization and proposition will actually make a profound difference to our income and profits.* That seems counter-intuitive; all business experts or modern business gurus will tell you to 'innovate and improve everywhere' or 'be constantly creative' or be left behind. But so-called 'improvements' and ongoing changes that we keep making, but are not reducing our stress and are not making us considerably more money – they ARE killing us. We have tried almost every tactic, everywhere, that we are told we should try. Therefore, challenge the Pareto principle's 20:80 rule and focus on the few percentages of problems and opportunities that will make all the difference.

*Consider for a minute that we may be fundamentally wrong about having to improve everywhere instead of dealing with reality: that most constraints – the core issues that are preventing you from achieving competitiveness in the*

marketplace – may arise, not because of a lack of innovativeness or 'creativity', but instead are due to inappropriate policy decisions or 'inappropriate boundaries between touch-points' in the supply chain that have been created in the past; *those* issues rather than the usual excuses and complaints about 'material' limitations?

This means that the solution to poor competitiveness must surely be easier to find and resolve than we think! *Decisions that confine and define structures and policies in our SMEs (and in our industry sectors!) produce limitations to what can be achieved, that are far in excess of any physical or operational boundaries.* Policies, especially those that cause constraints, underpin and intensify poor competitiveness and ill-thought-out improvements ultimately badly affect our ability to deliver to the market and be truly innovative.

## What are competitiveness and creativity, in terms of their use to me?

Being 'creative' and 'competitive' in the narrow context of simply being different is just not good enough. Competitiveness for the SME means being alone, not running with the pack nor being a 'me-too' follower of corporate improvement fashions or innovations. It means filling a real vacuum. Being 'creative' likewise isn't just about setting some time or budget aside to 'think outside the box' but it must change your product or proposition based on what the supply side wants (including both the product supply chain or any organizations or individuals that would have you make any change to your organization or its offerings). *Creativity is very much in the eye of the beholder and the beholder that matters is the one that is going to pay you good money for it.*

Being 'competitive' or 'creative' or indeed 'innovative' are just words unless they result in something ROBUST and ENDURING.

They must result in a superior position in the market, help create or shape a unique selling proposition of real value and not based on making your SME only different.

*Creativity and innovation are issues with striving to be different; competitive marketing empowers companies to make a real difference – for the consumer, customer and the company. It is not just about the new – or seeking the new – it is about 'unlearning' our past ways too... and we have to indelibly 'formalize' the process otherwise we will forget to ensure we remain competitive, consistently.*

# What SMEs think about competitiveness

There is a marked difference in all markets and industries between what marketing and competitiveness are considered to be, and what they could and should be for the SME. Consider the two very different attitudes shown in Table 3.1.

**TABLE 3.1**   Current thinking v SME enhanced competitiveness

| *Current* Thinking about Marketing and Competitiveness | What Marketing and Competitiveness *could and should be* for the SME |
|---|---|
| It is all about creating and projecting an embellished image about the company and its products | It is all about listening to and engaging with, the Prospect, Customer and Consumer |
| It is 'one-way shouting' at the Prospect, Customer or Consumer in as many ways and as loudly as possible, *distracting them and disturbing their lives* | Marketing offers two-way communications using a few compelling and focused methods to *engage* with others in a way that *enhances their lives* |
| Selling as much as we can of what we make or what we would wish to make (and make more of the same) | Better alignment of the needs of the market with the capabilities and competencies of the SME |
| Increasing the frequency and size of individual transactions | Maximizing the value of the relationship and income for our business and that of the Customer, whilst caring for the end consumer |
| Making 'shiny logos', brochures and other paraphernalia so that our company and products look attractive | Help make the SME or its whole Proposition more attractive whilst ensuring it is critical to the Customers' well being |
| Find new markets for existing products, persuading them to buy, and dropping customers afterwards whilst we try to find more | Find, engage and keep specific Customers who are likely to benefit most from and buy the current or modified product that makes most impact |

**TABLE 3.1**  *continued*

| *Current* Thinking about Marketing and Competitiveness | What Marketing and Competitiveness *could and should be* for the SME |
|---|---|
| Creating, expanding on, or embellishing any hint of a potential Unique Selling Point or Proposition that will make us look different in *any* way | Creating, offering and delivering a Proposition that is better received by the Customer and *cannot be readily matched* by the competition |
| A stress purchase; (as an SME I don't want to spend money on it) | An ongoing and consistent investment, creating and keeping Customers |
| To cajole the Prospect or Customer into enquiring or buying products that they may not otherwise buy or may buy elsewhere | To inform, listen and engage with the Prospect and Customer to ensure that we know their ongoing needs, now and in the future |
| Oversimplification and erroneous addiction to a product-focused culture (eg the old simplistic 'marketing mix') | Developing and embracing a systemic view of the supply chain, with a market-focused approach and process (eg adopting the modern marketing mix) |
| 'We don't do marketing'… 'It's only about promotions and advertising, isn't it?'… 'It costs far too much money, with little return'… etc. etc. | 'We understand marketing is the process of sensing and responding to the market, its position as the competitive "pulse" of our business, and an important *investment* in making and sustaining revenue' |
| We know what our competitive advantage is; we make some great stuff and all we need to do is find someone to buy it, or be persuaded to buy it | We know how to identify what our competitive advantage is, where it lies, how it can be fostered, and how we can continue to improve and modify it in a way that the market finds overwhelmingly appealing and valuable |

**TABLE 3.1**  *continued*

| *Current* Thinking about Marketing and Competitiveness | What Marketing and Competitiveness *could and should be* for the SME |
|---|---|
| We focus on controlling as much of our technical product manufacture as we can and the means with which to make it and our SME *efficient* | We control as many of the elements of the *entire* Proposition and make our SME constantly *effective* |
| We concentrate on getting a reasonable slice of the margin in the supply and sales chain | We concentrate on creating true value and are paid accordingly for value we create and deliver, rather than how much 'effort' we employ |
| We price and value our business proposition based on product margin, 'cost plus', what we think we can get, or the target price we need | We price our entire proposition based on what it precisely does for the Customer and embrace mutual profit that underpins this perspective |
| We flow with the next idea, fad, piece of advice, TLA initiative (Three Letter Acronym) and ongoing fire fighting that takes up our time each day | We stick to actions and activities that make us the most competitive organization that we can be and are seen to make a difference |
| **We focus on cost cutting and 'productivity' and the process of 'making the same things, better'** | **We focus on competitiveness, our position in the market and the process of nurturing our Customers and 'making better things'** |
| **We catch-up and react to the industry (using benchmarking etc.)** | **We sense, adapt to, and shape the market (agility)** |
| **Marketing is a waste of time, effort and money for the SME!!!!!** | *A 'revenue machine' to generate income for the business* |

© Copyright David James Hood: Competitive SME

# What marketing does for SME competitiveness

Stop and think for a minute about yourself and why *you* buy; each one of us is an individual customer too; we search, consider and buy a number of goods and services from others. What would you have those organizations and channels that provide you with products and services do to improve value sufficiently and make you a satisfied customer or consumer?

Would you really care whether your suppliers undertook this initiative or that, whether they had tens or thousands of customers, what systems they put in to help themselves make more money, etc? No, I am sure you would not.

'Marketing is the difference between "being merely different and making a real difference...".'

(David James Hood)

You probably would think that those companies would have improved only if what they actually offered to you was more akin to what you wished, when you wished it, in the form that you would have it delivered, and of course based on the value you would place on it. Likewise, your prospects, customers or consumers don't care much for your internal 'efficiencies' or improvement drives etc., *but they do care about whether your product can MAKE THEM MORE MONEY, SAVE THEM TIME, or make their LIVES MORE FRUITFUL AND HAPPY.*

You, as a customer or consumer, would not expect any less. So your customer or consumer must be thinking just like you; right? So what can marketing do to help your customer or consumer reach these objectives? How can marketing help them buy from you as opposed to another company or supplier?

- Realize that competitiveness – through marketing – gives you a superior proposition and position in the market based upon a 'true value proposition'.

- Marketing is the difference between 'being different and making a difference'; and avoid using 'solutions' and other vacuous words at all costs!

- Remember that the Business to Business (B2B) buyer in your supply chain *is not simply buying purchasing capability; he or she is buying operational capability for their organization.*

- Marketing can fundamentally get you away from the cost-trap and progress towards superior positioning and being paid better for the value you provide.

Remember: being competitive is much more than being creative or simply different; it is about being profoundly elegant in providing things that people and businesses find critical and important.

## Competitive SME and marketing

In fitting perfectly with the European Union futureSME initiative, this book helps the SME address the three main tenets as introduced in the first chapter; these components make up a highly focused and practical methodology to allow the SME to improve competitiveness. Those tenets are confronted and resolved in large part, through invigorated SME marketing capabilities.

**TABLE 3.2**  What marketing can do

| Tenet | What marketing can do |
| --- | --- |
| Strategy | Puts the market, customer and consumer at the heart of the business and is the foundation to building great strategies and revenue making capabilities |
| Adaptability | Provides the 'Sensing and Responding' process for the SME |
| Resilience | Gives the SME a more robust and sustainable advantage over longer periods of time |

© Copyright David James Hood: Competitive SME

## OK, so where do we start? – using the tools in this book

Now take a good look at what you currently have. Not in the usual way that you hear from some consultant suggesting 'lets go a few steps back and do a situation analysis', but a quick, honest and insightful look at where you *are* before moving on to where you *could be*.

Marketing offers us the means to gain this insight into our own business and how it can improve: it gives us the following POWERFUL yet practical and even *enjoyable* tools to unmistakably get the competitiveness process well underway:

- *SWOT* Analysis (strengths, weaknesses, opportunities and threats);
- *the marketing audit*;
- *the product (market) life cycle* – 'PLC';
- *market and marketing research*;
- *the value proposition & matrix*;
- *perceptual planning* (mapping out where we are or could be competitively positioned in the market);
- *the marketing mix* (the traditional 'Ps', now improved to reflect modern business);
- *branding for the SME*.

... and a few other things before we get to that *'unique selling proposition'* (the infamous USP we need to be competitive!):

- *a fantastic, real-world and insightful* account of how an SME can excel using a new marketing focus.

Then we finish the book with *two major and profound new ways to build sales and marketing capability and sales*, through greater engagement with your market.

Then you can work towards *'making to order'* and establishing true 'CRM'.[1]

These marketing topics will be examined, updated and expanded throughout the remainder of this book, but I would like to start by looking at the *marketing mix* and the *marketing audit*. We should perhaps, actually finish off the book with the marketing mix rather than mention it now, but it is necessary to understand what we are trying to translate and transcribe from good SME marketing practice into your whole proposition and it is well worthwhile clarifying the marketing mix now, before we move on to encouraging you to undertake your own marketing audit.

## The marketing mix

The marketing mix was also known as 'the four Ps', which most certainly fell well short of its mandate, which is to allow for the categorization of all the elements of the proposition and give us a template to create, improve and propel a proposition into the marketplace. Table 3.3 is simply used here to introduce you to the modern marketing mix; it not only addresses the shortfall of the initial mix, but also ensures that we have a full and thorough checklist to make sure your SME is poised and ready to deliver a competitive proposition.

**TABLE 3.3**  The marketing mix

| Marketing Mix Element | Description and Definition |
|---|---|
| **Product** *(original 'P')* | The main physical or core part of your proposition; the main value you are offering and delivering to your market through a 'vehicle' (see Chapter 7 on the constitution of the various components of a 'product') |
| **Promotion** *(original 'P')* | Usually tactical changes to campaigns and the proposition to allow for short term staging and projection based on a particular benefit, hook or other device to capture the interest and imagination of the customer or consumer and entice them to buy |
| **Place** *(original 'P')* | How and where your customer or consumer can find out about it, or purchase your product or service, and how and where it is delivered within the supply chain |
| **Price** *(original 'P')* | The monetary figure the customer or consumer pays you in exchange for the value you will, or have, delivered through supplying your product or service |
| **People and service** | *(Why was this missing from the initial '4 Ps' of marketing?)* This is everyone involved in getting the product or service created, developed, produced and delivered and who keep creating value for the market and for the organization; indeed this could be said to include all 'stakeholders', including the customer! |
| **Positioning** | Where your proposition or company is placed in terms of the *market's* perception of your value proposition, its relative value when the offer is compared to others, and how it is evidentially received in the market and in 'the mind of the prospect, customer and consumer' |
| **Project Management** | We are *all* project managers now; each campaign, tactic, activity, improvement or change needs careful planning and execution; unfortunately, this leads to multi-tasking and overlapping responsibilities! We all need to become first-rate Project Managers to ensure more efficient personal work patterns and effective delivery of our strategies and plans |

**TABLE 3.3** *continued*

| Marketing Mix Element | Description and Definition |
|---|---|
| **Profit** | The net cash we need to generate on the way to achieving our goal and purpose for the organization; something that needs to be fostered for *both* our organization *and* its customer base. The portion between 'turnover' or 'revenue' and our investments in 'operating expense and inventory' |
| **Process** | The coded and uncoded methods and procedures that are physical, intellectual, intangible and now digital, used to enable us to run effectively as an organization and supply to our market |
| **Priority** | Ensuring at all times that our decisions and activities are based on removing primary constraints on ourselves (the company) and our customers (the market), AT THE EXCLUSION of other options that are not addressing core issues and when resolved must maximize returns and outputs for the whole of our 'business system'. *A good prioritization process can markedly reduce stress for the SME and its key people and improve management attention* |
| **Policy** | The established vision, purpose, principles and accompanying guidelines and structures that we work to in our organization, that allow us to best exploit and benefit from true customer and market 'centricity' and help secure common profit |
| **Physical evidence** | Instead of simply 'being creative or innovative' we ensure that all of our changes, both in terms of their substance and priority, are made on the basis of keeping firmly in line with our **Priority**-making process and that evidence leads us to create better products, services and propositions based on market needs and meeting those needs to best effect, to create **Profit** |
| **Precision** | To gain the maximum ROI from our efforts, and to optimize how we get to those who would wish to buy our products and services, we need to be precise in how we sense, engage with and serve the market. Great marketing is key to reducing waste and maximizing return for our efforts |

**TABLE 3.3**  *continued*

| Marketing Mix Element | Description and Definition |
| --- | --- |
| Pervasiveness | The extent to which our organization truly subscribes to the main tenets of marketing and our people buy in to the concept of marketing, customer-centricity and our personal efforts to 'progress through competitive marketing' |
| Pleasant | Good corporate responsibility and governance are now a given; unfortunately good delivery and customer service is not. We need to make sure that all our intentions and activities are enacted in good faith as citizens and representatives of our organization and likewise our organizations 'walk-the-walk' when it comes to being good corporate citizens, treating all fairly and honestly |
| Pivot | How we ensure that all our efforts concentrate on the customer in the market; this involves having a Champion at top level in the business who continually ensures that we have a real, consistent and meaningful customer focus |

# The marketing audit

We truly need to know where we are – through the eyes, not of the accountant, advisor, consultant (or family member or friend) but *through the eyes of the prospect, customer or consumer.*

(For convenience, the marketing audit questions are to be found within the appendices at the back of this book. Listed below are some of the important, and very much overlooked, aspects of marketing that will be revealed through a simple marketing audit.)

Take a good look at the following questions, answer them honestly by placing your answers on the accompanying 'Likert scales'. Try to answer these questions as frankly as possible (and include views of your colleagues and your market too); you can use these important findings along with other tools in the following chapters to help refine your competitive advantage by comparing and calibrating your responses now with any positive change you make in the future. Each of these questions requires a simple response along a Likert-scale. (Note that these scales all have *EVEN* number gradations, so that one is forced to choose and not 'take the easy, middle option'!)

*Each question offers a statement or question; the scale prompts you to comment on how your organization is performing and instead of using normal conventions such as 'strongly agree' and 'strongly disagree', short descriptors have been used to help you make your decision.*

It is worthwhile quickly completing this marketing audit process quickly *now*, before you read through the rest of this book; once you have read on and compiled your own comprehensive plan to increase your competitiveness (and worked through any other activities identified by the futureSME initiative on your strategy map if applicable), you can use these questions again as a robust means to check your new improved position against where you were when you first read this book.

Later, you can use the audit to help calibrate ongoing improvements and to help sustain your competitive advantage by adding other questions that reflect the proposition and delivery key success factors that come from continuing and completing the path set out in this book.

## Quick marketing audit

(© Copyright David James Hood: Competitive SME)

- How well do you know your *immediate* customer? (We will return to this, so don't worry; just note your initial response.)

**FIGURE 3.1**

- How well do you know your end-user customer or consumer?

- Are our product and service improvements and any major changes based mainly on internal or market input?

**FIGURE 3.2**

- We have adopted a pricing policy that best reflects the market's needs and the customer-evidenced idea of value.

**FIGURE 3.3**

- Price confidence level: how confident are we that we have set the best price that reflects our value to the market?

**FIGURE 3.4**

- In terms of 'people-hours', how much time do our customer-facing staff spend proportionately between internal meetings and external conversations?

**FIGURE 3.5**

- How happy are you that your brand is 'positioned' – what your market thinks about you – and well placed in the market?

**FIGURE 3.6**

- Like most organizations, we have options as to where and how to communicate and promote to our customers; do we only try a few marketing channels, or as many as possible?

**FIGURE 3.7**

Very few channels | 1 2 3 4 5 6 7 8 | Many different channels

- We consistently and constantly review and update our publications – that is, all the brochures, websites, sales literature etc – 'to try and keep our market up to date' with our messages and latest proposition announcements.

**FIGURE 3.8**

Never review 'publications' | 1 2 3 4 5 6 7 8 | Review consistently always

- We speak to our customers or consumers post-purchase and place them firmly within an after-sales plan (or schedule in at least a number of calls or contact opportunities to keep them informed and engaged)

**FIGURE 3.9**

Only follow up for more sales | 1 2 3 4 5 6 7 8 | Strict follow up in a post sale plan

- We use a feedback system, or at least record any customer feedback that we receive *other than* using a production quality system (such as Six Sigma).

**FIGURE 3.10**

No formal recording system | 1 2 3 4 5 6 7 8 | Have a formal feedback system

● We include our customers and prospects in our product improvement and development process on a structured basis.

**FIGURE 3.11**

Do not involve customers in new products | 1 2 3 4 5 6 7 8 | Intimately involve customers in new products

● We follow up on all customer or consumer complaints with a resolution and ensure they are satisfied.

**FIGURE 3.12**

Follow up only to save the sale | 1 2 3 4 5 6 7 8 | Follow up resolutely 'and beyond'

● Have we identified all people – internally and externally – that are involved in any and all customer-facing, 'value adding' contact with the product or customer and manage, train and resource them accordingly?

**FIGURE 3.13**

We only consider obvious 'front facing', staff | 1 2 3 4 5 6 7 8 | We have identified all involved in market contact

● Do we have a designated person or people for the role of marketing and ensuring 'constant and consistent contact' with the market?

**FIGURE 3.14**

Marketing and market contact is ad-hoc | 1 2 3 4 5 6 7 8 | Designated roles for marketing and contact

- Where do we lie on the scale from reliability to response? Do we care more about quality processes and getting production of the product more efficient', or have a greater focus on responsiveness to customers and the market?

**FIGURE 3.15**

- How long has my recognized competitive advantage lasted in the market recently?

**FIGURE 3.16**

**FIGURE 3.17**    Summary of the essentials from this chapter

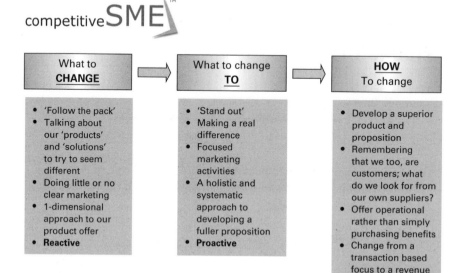

**FIGURE 3.18**   Chapter 3 summary action table

| ☑ | CHAPTER 3 Summary Action Table |
|---|---|
| ☐ | Realize that only a FEW issues underpin your inability to meet new challenges and opportunities head-on |
| ☐ | Realize and convey to all your Team that it is no good to strive to be *different*, we have to make a *difference* |
| ☐ | Check the Marketing and Competitiveness Table for the SME and discuss this with your Team; translate onwards, and using their words get them to describe what each point will mean for each of their individual roles and operations |
| ☐ | Make a firm commitment – not only to use the list of tools outlined in this Chapter as part of your plans to improve, but set aside a calendar date now with the Team to do workshop sessions with them, one workshop for each tool |
| ☐ | Go through the existing Marketing Mix with your Board and Team; get feedback, comments and ideas; they will help in your plan of action to improve competitiveness |
| ☐ | Do the Marketing Audit with your Team; assess if you or the Team would wish to add any further questions |

© Copyright David James Hood: Competitive SME

*It isn't just about finding and filling a gap in the market; it is about filling in an unacceptable and important vacuum where a true customer need remains unfulfilled.*

DAVID JAMES HOOD

## Note

**1** We will deal with 'CRM' – customer relationship management – later; suffice to say that the heart of true CRM is in offering the SME the ability to reduce the risk associated with making to stock, and progressing toward what is called here 'making to order'. In realizing that making to stock is a necessary activity for many SMEs, the emphasis we suggest should change as when one garners a greater understanding of the market and customer need, then timing of the creation and delivery of products and services should be optimized and hence reduce the need for copious stock levels. Simply put, reducing stock by knowing what the customer needs and when, over and above what your competitors know, can reduce the need to hold stock and taking the risk of creating something that may not sell quickly or at all.

# Increasing your confidence
## Leveraging what you have

> *Man is small, and, therefore, small is beautiful.* EF SCHUMACHER

You are reading this book, so you are well on your way to creating a sustainable edge. However, the reality is that many of us in SMEs simply do not have the confidence to become what we could be. Well, rest assured that although you hear from many 'advisors' that the magic elixir of power and productivity is always achievable – as long as you buy into their way of doing things of course – real prowess is within your grasp. There is nothing glib in realizing that whatever you do, whatever your resources or personal and company capabilities, you will always have the means to create something worthy, long standing and different.

You can create and build something so entirely different and attractive that your customer and market will readily appreciate and grasp it with both hands, whilst your competitors are stuck in their own mire of self-doubt and fire-fighting, frustrated at how you are doing so well. They will continue as usual – wasting their money and effort innovating everywhere and anywhere at the hope of betterment, whilst you focus your efforts on improvement that really matters.

## Affordability

I would personally rather take on the services of a good copywriter than a marketing or advertising agency. I would rather create messages that can be 'targeted and delivered by sniper' to a distinctive, selected (preferably self-selected) audience than blast my message anywhere and everywhere in the hope that someone will hear, or that some of it will stick. As SMEs, we cannot afford waste. We cannot afford to spend time and money on telling our messages to people and organizations with whom we will do no business.

## SME\ The power of 'FREE'

Quite a lot of what we can do positively, in engaging with our market, is free – or almost free. That said, my caveat is that in addition to the saying that nothing of course is truly free, our precious resource that is time certainly is not. We can, though, look at various free and low-cost methods to get our messages out, to engage with our market audience and increase our footprint and profile in the market. This is of particular interest and importance to those of us who have or manage SMEs with limited, precious, budgets.

That is where we can gain a major advantage on big business: our ability to be interesting to others, to be *extremely specific and personal*. We surprisingly can have rather a lot to say; we have an opinion that can be important and often have a real insight to share. We do have a lot of information and intelligence that may not be principally ours but that we have access to and that may be of genuine interest to our market.

Remember that most knowledge we accumulate and information or content that we can provide is relatively free. Indeed, accumulating information from your market in the form of a survey is relatively low cost too, the results of which can be shared by your prospect and customer communities. We have of course spent time, effort – and money – gaining that 'intellectual property' but to collate it and put it into bite-sized pieces to share with the market is relatively low cost. We now need to ensure that we impart that knowledge to the marketplace, again at low relative cost and seeking maximum return. (For example, e-mailing or posting an article, personally, to important customers as you think it may be interesting to them will surprise; it is astonishing how little this single and sometimes very cheap engagement approach is used.)

## Communicate, communicate, communicate

Think about those multiple channels or communities where your markets congregate. At the trade exhibition, at the sub-group of a trade or professional membership body and now online in 'social' groupings (more on those later) – the opportunity to engage with our market has expanded exponentially. The need for information – or better still, supplying good intelligence and critical knowledge for your customers and consumers – is becoming less of a nice-to-have and now more of a necessity. They want to be able to sort out 'information' from the real 'insights and intelligence'... so help them. Just because there is more information does not necessarily mean they will be better off for receiving it!

*'Storytelling is the most powerful way to put ideas into the world today'.*

(Robert McKee)

We can record podcasts, interviews and video clips, create ads, blogs and e-mail, and touch many people, at relatively little cost. Remember – those who wish to know about you, the 'chattering classes' in your industry, who talk incessantly about your industry such as trade publication editors and feature writers, exhibition organizers, radio and TV producers, webcast-event hosts, journalists and a host of others actually need your input – *they actively welcome and want your 'stories'* or snippets of knowledge and insights. Indeed, they may even want you personally (such as a speaker at an event) – a golden opportunity to put your 'story' out, in person.

Likewise, you could invite many prospects, customers, consumers and 'chattering class influencers' to an event hosted at your location; offer work-shops and educational insights. All the people listed above have a job to do and want help in doing it – so give away your messages and your personal time to those who would help put you in front of your market. They can help you build your personal profile and that of your SME. Indeed, you can and should build your own personal brand as 'trustworthy', 'knowledge-able', gaining and mastering a reputation as someone that any editor, reporter, exhibitor, conference organizer or feature writer will instantly contact if they have some issue relating to your speciality or marketplace. Moreover of course, these priceless contacts should be in your CRM system and constantly and consistently fed with snippets of your knowledge and opinions reinforcing you as a key driver and leader in your market.

And remember, if you *do* have to pay for any kind of promotional activity, *never pay the rate card*. There is always a deal to be had to get your objectives met. A bit of creative thinking and pressure applied to the media owner or agent may be needed perhaps, but they ultimately will want to take your money. It is always a good thought to ponder when negotiating – they always want your money and may do a lot more than you think to get their hands on it. Remember also that they have to prove return on investment to YOU; you are taking a huge gamble that you will get the message across, or more importantly secure the necessary action from the recipient; you need assurances about *ROI* and not just pleasantries and technicalities about 'how many column inches' or other such description of what you are buying. *You are buying returns*, not items or space, or enquiries; you wish purchases not 'exposure', 'eyeballs' or 'clicks'. Drive a hard bargain; you will always be able to go elsewhere to reach the same or an equally valuable audience.

SME\

*These 'chattering classes' and communities all have an audience – and very often much larger than the one you have on your database or have direct access to.*

They want your stories – and you can create and give those carefully crafted stories or themes to them. Just ask; I have on occasion secured great value for very little relative effort, including tens of thousands of pounds and euros worth of exhibition stands, space, exposure, 'column inches' and interaction purely because I made sure I had something interesting to say. If I can do it by myself, you can do it with your similarly 'limited' SME budget and resources. But only if what you give in return is of value to those whose help you are seeking.

Create a large database of worthies – the communicators in your business and industry. E-mail them regularly with good intelligence and insights; do not limit it to information about product launches and items that you may consider worthy, as they will just see that as you merely promoting your product. Ask journalists what they are currently researching, for example, as a good means to encourage two-way conversations; remember, as with your prospects and customers, two way communication is essential for success with those who like to talk about the 'goings on' in your market.

Remember, 'free' is not just about giving or receiving something for nothing. You will have to put something into any activity to make it worthwhile and work for you and your organization. It is all about making sure that any effort pays off and focuses your time and hard-earned budget on gaining a specific return.

# Piggyback

As the term suggests, utilize the resources of others to help you achieve your objectives – but do so in a way that achieves theirs too! An example given earlier is the use of exhibitions; you could tie up with larger companies, industry publishers and supply-chain partners, almost anyone with whom you could reciprocate some value. What can you give them? Well, it depends on your knowledge of your customer and market, your 'personal brand' and on considering and completing the remainder of this chapter...

# 'I just don't have anything to say'

Very often, what stops us making the best impression and impact on our market is that we think we do not have a good issue to communicate to our audience. In trying to stay away from using hyperbole, or to stop ourselves simply making up a story or feature just because we have to sell our product and anything we communicate would appear glib and obvious or boring, we remain frustrated and quiet.

 *'As a small business person, you have no greater leverage than the truth'.*

(Paul Hawken)

*There is always something to say.* Remember the old adage that 'any publicity is good publicity' (although it patently is not!). There is resonance in that phrase however; the market needs to know about you and you about it. You are in the market, you are part of it; people should care about what you are doing to help them fulfil their needs – but only if you make your messages and 'stories' relevant and meaningful.

 *Dyson's success wasn't just based on good design – it was a FANTASTIC story.*

Remember: nobody knows more about your market, its place and potential within it, and cares about both of those related issues, than you can. No generic industry report, competitor activity or comment from the industry 'chattering classes' can or should determine what you create in product, proposition or communication terms. It is really all about your personal or organizational credibility, your ability to uncover the needs of the market, your success at engaging and your conduct within it.

 *'Facts tell;
stories sell.'*

*This is where an SME can excel*; although big business has its seemingly endless departments, executives, big budgets, power and agencies, the SME can have the main and powerful elements for a profoundly terrific story:

- Trust and capability (how often have big businesses been accused of an uncaring attitude towards customers?).

- Sincerity (people like to hear about small companies and the 'small person' succeeding).

- It isn't all about battling for size of market or market share; it is about the importance of your SME within it.

- Big businesses have to care more about their shareholders, 'the city' and the industry chattering classes; the SME cares mainly about its customers and consumers.

- Because the SME could be said to be more agile and adaptable than the large company (indeed that is a core precept of the futureSME initiative) you can comment and engage with the market more readily as it inherently knows SMEs often lead the way in innovation.

- It can be very cheap to push and promote the story (eg using press releases, features, appearances, even posting cards that carry a brief story, rather than expensive brochures with too much information).

Of course, you may even have some very willing, happy customers that would help you with your 'story', telling of some real understanding that you showed towards their needs and wants (but keep away from too specific case-study-type blandness!)

## SME\ So what makes a great story?

Whatever form your communication takes, whether it is a letter, brochure, website page, blog or e-mail, the fundamentals remain much the same. If it does not 'sizzle' then it will not grab attention!

Check your situation using some of the tools contained in this book; they should give you food for thought regarding what could be a good story, an interesting and attention-grabbing message for the market.

The following pages offer guidance to set up your own 'promotional story'; in addition to providing you with some key insights into your own business and proposition, they could be used as a template to offer a brief to any outside agents or promotional partners or platform you employ to help get your product or proposition out into the marketplace. Try out the process shown in Figure 4.1: the 'communications loop'.

**FIGURE 4.1** The communications loop

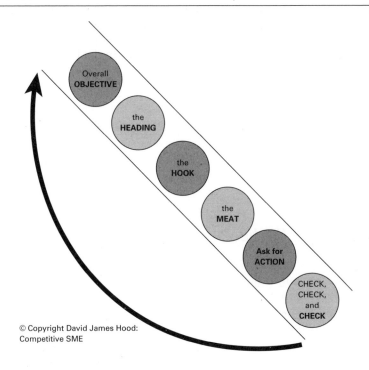

© Copyright David James Hood: Competitive SME

## The objective for the 'story'

The objective should be clearly worked out before you start your story or promotional activity. It is clear that you wish to make money; but you also want to ensure that you cover the stages necessary to get action from your market that leads to a sale. Remember, that at all times you are warming up your audience or reader to perform an action, and that you are brand-building in the most fundamental yet potent way because you are telling a real story.

## Heading

The heading is obviously an important component of your 'story'. However, it is also the one where the most fundamental mistakes can be made. There is a tendency to go for the mundane, the cliché, the grandiose or the downright boring. What you need is something that reflects the buyer's perspective and context. When the prospect, customer or consumer is exposed to your story, *they need to see themselves in the heading*; their challenges, opportunities, thoughts, perceptions and whether you are going to help them gain something, or conversely, reduce or get rid of some problem for them.

This is true of any representation of your 'story' – from a short article in a trade magazine to a personal presentation at a seminar. You have to grab attention and engage a person's brain; that of course is necessary, but insufficient... you need to keep their attention with a quick statement about 'WIFM' – 'what's in it for me?' And that leads us to the hook...

'Creativity is thinking up new things. Innovation is doing new things'.

(Theodore Levitt)

## Introduction: the hook

At this stage, it would be wise to consult the 'Steps to changing your value proposition' section in the book (Chapter 7) in preparation for creating a piece of engaging content or a theme.

The 'hook' is not just some glib and recognized means to gain attention; it has to be a real and strong message or primary connection with the audience, so that they are not left thinking 'what is this all about' or worse, 'so what?' One sees so many stories about SMEs 'doing this and that' or achieving some award or adopting some internal change, which is really no more than the SME writing to and for, themselves; instead of using a great opportunity to connect and hook their market, they squander it by talking about their own business and concerns.

'Ask yourself, always, whilst composing a message or proposition for your market: "which means that..." or "so what?" to every feature, benefit or phrase you think is important – it may not be to your prospect or customer.'

That is why they are reading – to gain a benefit or reduce a problem. *Believe me, the customers or consumers don't give a fig about you or how wonderful you are; they have problems, aspirations, issues, ideas, needs and wants, and if they cannot see those being attended to and quickly in your story, then bid them goodbye!* They will not look, listen, read, or wish to try to absorb anything that is in effect, interrupting their lives. In our modern, time-starved world, we cannot afford the time to waste and neither can your prospect, customer or consumer; do not assume they have time to spend on your communications; they may not even want them. However if the hook is substantive and actually meaningful, then you are doing everyone a favour.

## The 'meat'

Remember, as always, whom you are targeting with the marketing 'story' or activity. It is easy to forget that when creating some good marketing pieces, such as adverts, we wrongly try not only to make the proposition attractive but also not to exclude anyone who may buy. So we tend to forget that we do not want to target any type of buyer, but only the ones who are most likely to benefit from our proposition and likely to actually purchase it. So we can waste valuable time and budget investment in revenue generation, trying to 'make things pretty' rather than effective.

The 'meat' of your piece should be valuable in its own right; it is not enough to create selling messages in the 'meat' of any communication. You must give the reader or recipient a good reason to look or listen to your message, but also engage that person with important and valuable content. *Intelligent intelligence, not indifferent information.* This is a reality of the new, digitally enabled revolution. People turn off readily if they consider any communications to be some blatant selling mechanism or find the content uninspiring and – worse – irrelevant. The information in any message of communication with your customer or consumer must be critical, or at least informative, interesting and even entertaining.

(See further notes on improving communication in Chapter 12: Optimizing your proposition and making more money.)

 ## Action – ask the recipient to actually DO SOMETHING

Surprisingly, but understandably, the action one would wish the recipient to do is often left unclear, or indeed missing entirely! Once you have crammed in so many features, ideas, taglines and selling 'puff' you can forget to ask the recipient of your message to actually DO SOMETHING. Look at some adverts or other communications or messages – there is a formula for most – and they generally end with a reference to the product, how to get it, how much it costs or some other main reason for buying it, and then an instruction as to WHAT YOU SHOULD DO NOW.

You can spend a lot of time and money on getting those messages in front of the intended recipient – so make sure you get return on that investment by asking them to do something – ALWAYS.

It is not enough to 'put the brand in their head' or to have any other woolly objective than to ask them to do something. I am fed up with the 'yes we don't ask them to buy or do anything, as we are trying to improve our brand and get share of mind...' blah-de-blah. Advertising agencies and others will tell you lots of things so that you will not take them to task when your ads and other activities do not result in real returns for you – results that you can actually place in the *bank*.

You should always have a firm idea about what your message or piece of communication should *convey*, but equally what you wish the recipient to *do*. It must lead to something further; not only the obvious 'buy now' – it could be anything from a competition entry, to update their details on your system, to enquire about a trial – anything – but it shouldn't just be 'for information only', even if you are 'indulging' in a brand-building exercise or trying to raise your profile. If it is, then you should not send it. It should be of value; it need not always result in someone sending you money directly, but it should help them make money or improve their lives. *The same can be said about the message as for the product* – if it does not lead to saving time, saving or making money or improving their lives, then it is not of value.

## SME\ *Check, check and check again...*

Does the message or communication piece develop and maintain your company brand – how your company and proposition is supported and represented in story, logo, colour, essence, and match clearly to the new message, article or feature that your are creating? Remember, that in addition to ensuring that your new message results in some immediate impact, the continuing legacy it produces will add to your brand and perception of your proposition and company in the market – so it must be consistent with your brand and the essence of your overall strategy and purpose. (We cover the 'brand' later in Chapter 7).

Do not be scared to change components for different audiences and perform trial campaigns or messages; whilst it is preferable to steer clear of 'tweaking' with the proposition, each market segment will probably need changes to the proposition and the 'story' you have constructed, as the 'brand' will require some modification and refinement depending on the receiving target audience.

## 'Roots for reception'

Make sure that your communication covers the *'roots for reception'*, ensuring that it is clear, relevant and will be welcome:

- It contains *visuals* – diagrams or images that powerfully and clearly convey what you wish to convey (do not use generic stock photos!).
- It tells a good '*story*' – some people like to 'see' things (illustrations and graphical symbols), others prefer to 'hear' (within any dialogue, they like descriptions), and others like to be 'shown' (they like the demonstration, the video, the hands-on trial or process explained).

If you tell a story, then tell it in a way that your audience would wish to be shown, covering all these three types, so that they all enjoy and understand your message.

- It evokes the *senses* – what would someone hear from another person that may help? A good example of this is testimonials – the bedrock of good word-of-mouth and developing trust in you, your proposition and your brand. You should be writing pieces of succinct prose. Think Churchill or Martin Luther King. They knew how to sell.

- It contains '*power words*' and phrases – remember, every word as well as image, sound, etc has to work and work well; nothing should be extra 'filling'. Every word should evoke feelings and interest. It is easy to find power words – just Google for some. Also, look at what other good adverts or pieces of promotional material say. Less is more. Those words have to be powerful. And of course, relevant!

- Always ask at every appropriate opportunity for a testimonial, to add to your story (or better still, get the happy customer or consumer to write a short story for you!).

## Supporting 'slogans'

If you chose to create and use a slogan or 'tag line' – make it meaningful. I cannot believe some of the slogans and taglines used by business. They often include bland words such as 'quality' (please avoid using this word – it does not mean anything at all) and some similarly bland statements or some spurious aspiration, characteristics (that the product does not have), or promise (that the product is unlikely to fulfil).

It does not matter what size or heritage the company has – look at ICI, one of the largest branded chemical manufacturers in the world; their slogan was – 'World Class'. OK, you may think that at least this has merit because it is somewhat brief; but it is hardly memorable, specific or interesting. It does not convey what ICI could do for the market; they should have asked themselves the 'which means that...' question to explore and define what they should have said as a slogan, strap or tagline, to complement the product. Contrast the ICI slogan with Linn, a company that makes premium sound systems; their slogan is 'making everything sound better' or 'makes anything you listen to at home, sound better'. It tells the market precisely what to expect and what need is served.

*'It should not be about customer loyalty but our loyalty to the customer.'*

Ask yourself, when you review everything before using your new message, story or article: if you were to read this for the first time and thought 'which means that...' or if you are feeling particularly abrupt and unforgiving to yourself, 'so what?', to all your key elements of your story or message, this should act as a good b*******t remover and ensure that your message packs a real punch.

*Ask for feedback for the individual communication piece whenever you can – and commit to using it properly.*

## How you can actually use feedback to be a major differentiator

Let us get one thing straight: in the current business climate that continues to enthuse about 'customer relationship management' (CRM), a number of precepts are wholly wrong. No customer or consumer I have spoken with wants to be managed, nor do they really wish to feed in to a self-serving company database (especially now, when data protection prevails and individual's suspicions are aroused at being asked for their personal details and preferences); they do not really want to have a 'relationship' with any company at all.

The prospect or customer (and increasingly the consumer) sees the organization's attempts at data solicitation and capture as wholly self-serving and not necessarily conducted with their interest in mind. CRM – apart from it being another grotesque three letter acronym – mainly consists of 'sticking customer information into a database so that we can send many more messages to them and interrupt their lives more and more efficiently'.

*Do not just place any feedback from your 'exposure' and 'stories' into your 'process' to make things better for you and your delivery; it can and should form the backbone of any new or incremental product or proposition improvement.*

Managing relationships – or more appropriately, optimizing relevant contact and valuable engagement with your market – should be more about *effectiveness*. It should not be simply about efficiencies or a cynical means to help you more efficiently 'tell, yell and sell'. Neither is it about 'increasing customer loyalty'. How often have we heard that oft-used and horrendous phrase in business? *It should not be about customer loyalty but our loyalty to the customer. That must come first.* And that helps us tell really powerful stories.

**FIGURE 4.2**   Chapter 4 summary action table

| ☑ | CHAPTER 4 Summary Action Table |
|---|---|
| ☐ | Start to write some stories; give yourself some time to relax, think and create short stories about what it is you provide and what challenges you sort and what opportunities that you open up for your market |
| ☐ | Get some others, particularly those who work at the interface with the customer, to write stories; check them with yours and consolidate |
| ☐ | Make a list of the great and the good in your marketplace; these should include some close customers, commentators, journalists etc and ask them to take a look at some of your more refined stories – ask for feedback to ensure that your stories 'sizzle' |
| ☐ | Acquire and keep a diary or notebook specifically to list of any good subjects and experiences you have daily that could make for a great story; eg customer comments, things overhead at an event etc |
| ☐ | Feedback to the customer facing Team the above and go through the Communications Loop with them and get their feedback, buy-in and volunteers to set in place a managed, ongoing process |
| ☐ | Begin to use the 'Which Means That' test with the Team to refine some key messages for the 'stories', articles and any tagline or slogans you are considering |

© Copyright David James Hood: Competitive SME

**FIGURE 4.3**   Summary of the essentials from this chapter

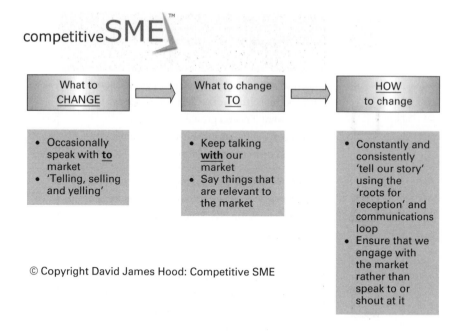

© Copyright David James Hood: Competitive SME

> *If you are not taking care of your customer, your competitor will.*

**BOB HOOEY**

# Maximizing SME management

## Making better decisions: Investments and predictions

> *There has been too much effort improving productivity focusing on the bottom line and ignoring the top line.*
>
> **PROF UMIT BITITCI, DIRECTOR, FUTURESME**

## What is 'success' in managing an SME?

This is a really good question; arguably it is what you determine and define it could and should be, and not what is conventionally described and understood: the successful drive to make more, do more, have more, and have more people doing it. Success is not about more, it is about satisfying our fellow human beings and ourselves in the process, *profitably*. It is a challenge to try and resist the temptation to consider success as 'taking over the world', 'getting 2 per cent of the global market' or 'growth for growth's sake'. Make your targets more 'granular' – how much, where, when, how to gain them and the main needs you wish to serve, from the market inwards.

 ## Knowing your direction, goals and objectives

The basis for making these decisions is knowing the difference between what is simply information or interesting data, and what is actual intelligence and critical data. There is more on this in Chapter 7 'Real Market Presence'. This helps build confidence that not only can you have a great story to tell; you can make a worthwhile impact on your market when you send or receive intelligence, helping you towards achievement of your revenue goal and how to get there (your objectives).

# Making decisions that matter

Visions, missions, mission statements, etc are all very well; but what our SME should be, where we should focus, what markets we are or should be in, what we should create and serve up and how we engage with that market are all more important questions and these are primarily marketing issues.

Most SMEs are very much driven by trial-by-tactic, and therefore not strategy led. Strategy and acting in a 'strategic way' with 'strategic intent' is not just for the large company. You would be surprised if you knew just how many SMEs 'don't do strategy' (or say they don't 'do' marketing as well!). That is why many SMEs – indeed most SMEs, including our own if we were honest with ourselves – ebb and flow *following the market rather than driving it.*

This frankly reflects the limiting condition that many SMEs do not have a clear vision, mission statement and goals; and these manifest themselves as no sharp and definitive partnership strategies, product creation plans, business development paths, intermediate short-term objectives or USP, and no market development and penetration or campaigning plans. It all distils down from a lack of a clear strategy.

As managers and owners who have to make key decisions about 'improvements and change', it is much more important to know strategically what to do at any point in time, than just to know more and more about faddish alternative technologies and tactical tweaks – the latter is what you could do. Its is much more important of course, to know precisely what you should do.

Making the right decisions – those that release the constraint from your business and result in liberating resources, funds, exploiting opportunities and determine where and how they will be *best* exploited – is critical to success for the SME. We always fall foul of looking within; letting our day-to-day fire-fighting and internal constraints produce hurdle after hurdle, tactic after tactic, so we cannot see where the money could or should be coming from nor formulate any long-term plans. Inward-looking fixations do not lead to comprehensible strategies, missions or decisiveness and making good, clear decisions.

*That is where marketing steps in*; it is the 'defining pulse for the best business approach to competitiveness'. Indeed at the heart of the futureSME aspiration for SMEs to achieve some form of agility and resilience, is the market; no business decision is complete without involving your market and external environment. Making better decisions, and concentrating on which decision should be taken, makes sense; the best and arguably the most important decision to be made, is what your whole proposition – your product and all the elements surrounding it – should constitute.

Deming and others champion the idea to 'eliminate the need for inspection and build quality into the product in the first place'. *Good competitive marketing practice however, emphasizes that we must build the right product or service in the first place.* Thus eliminating the need for wasteful campaigns and 'brow-beating the market into submission' and creating only what the market needs and what will be welcomed and profitable.

The following conflict shows us why it is patently clear that it is difficult to do both. Whilst we wish to remain 'lean' and able to be responsive to change, we still have to make assumptions and predictions as to what and when the market will buy (or we are able to sell in sufficient quantities).

*It is almost impossible to both manufacture our goods ahead of being able to sell them and yet await the order to ensure that we can supply exactly what the customer orders and when they need it (market demand).* Indeed, we would rather make them only when we have the order – to lower our inventory costs and allow for greater customization and satisfaction. It is especially difficult to risk building large amounts of stock given the rate of alternative competitive options in the market for the important customer, product obsolescence and changing customer needs. A dilemma indeed for the SME, with its limited resources! The problem is exacerbated by the fact that as the logic of the illustration demonstrates we do indeed *try* to do both.

We do one, when we would wish to do the other (Figure 5.1).

**FIGURE 5.1**   The barrier to adaptability and agility

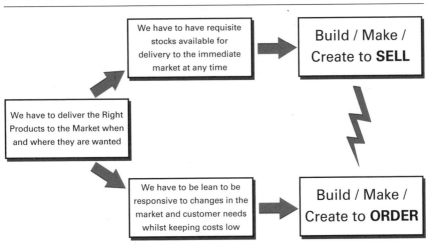

© Copyright David James Hood:
Competitive SME

We will have to break this 'cloud' or 'conflict' if we are ever to ensure that we achieve the goal in the main box observed on the left of the figure. We will attempt to 'break this cloud' in the course of this book and through the Competitive SME initiative. Ultimately, we know in our hearts that we must 'have requisite stocks' and also 'be lean and be responsive to change', but we would naturally prefer to 'make to order' or 'demand' rather than have warehouses and supply chains so full of stock, or have resourced up and created service that may not move with sufficient speed or indeed move at all. To be able to change from 'build/make to sell' to 'build/make to order' and therefore become truly agile, we need to address some fundamental issues about how we see the marketplace, how we engage with it and how we position ourselves within in. This book offers major steps in that direction. (See Chapter 10: Grasping the Opportunity: Sales, about the change to make to order/demand.)

In order to make a start in addressing the above conflict, we need to look at why we have this problem in the first place; we need to ask ourselves the following assumptions and test them:

- Why is it that we need to have a requisite stock level that feels disproportionately high and available at any time?

- Why is there such a long lead time to get a product into the hands of those who would benefit from its utility?

- Why do we have too many units of one product whilst having too few of another?

- How can we be ready for change, when we have to plan many months in advance and still may have to change strategies or tactics that would therefore be difficult or nigh on impossible?

- Why is it that we build products that have to be sold at a lower price than anticipated or actually become almost obsolete, even before we have had a chance to clear them from stock or make some real returns from them?

- How can we, in reality, keep our costs at their lowest without causing problems with current delivery and yet improve, innovate and invest in improvement at the same time?

- Do we have to make items now and take such a gamble by betting our investments on future market needs and trends yet hoping that we can change later when it is necessary and will know exactly when to change and what changes to make?

- *Are our traditional measurements, how we determine, predict, control and supply actually preventing us from resolving the conflict?*

- *Is there anything we can do to keep our stocks low, our product configuration options wider, our investment returns higher, our response times better, our sensing and responding capabilities more accurate and effective, and our overall product proposition more valued – indeed almost critical – to our market?*

The answer to the last question begins with the formation of your appropriate strategy. We need to have a strategy that sets out how we will address these issues, become a 'make to order' organization and to align our organization's interests with those of the market. Without good, true two-way marketing at the heart of both our strategy and operations, we will continue to suffer from the above conflict and our interests will never be synchronized with the market. So how can we break the conflict and start to address these aspirations?

 Both the demands and interests of the organization must align with those of the market. (See Chapter 8 on marketing planning.)

## Strategy

No dialogue or discovery about breaking the above conflict, improving marketing and competitiveness can continue without first establishing a formal strategy. Building, resourcing, making, selling, servicing and ordering are all marketing and market activities and considerations so we need to start and end with a strategy that has the market 'centre-stage'.

Marketing is often not seen as a strategic activity, but rather a tactical means to react to the market and a 'necessary evil'. The result of this error means that marketing is usually smacked on the back of the planning and strategy processes and as such is an afterthought; and the opportunity to get marketing right – and likewise the product and proposition configured as it should be for maximum gain – is significantly lessened right from the start. An irony indeed for an activity that is said to be worth, in value terms, *three times more than any other activity to the business*. It is hidden away and regarded as a tactical unwanted and 'expensive' irritation!

 We cannot move towards building/making to order until we stop building/making to sell and start to listen more attentively to the market and work from the outside, inwards. Place marketing – not just 'the market', but also the actual *process* – as a core part of our STRATEGY.

*The good news? Well, you can address this readily; it is easier than you think and the methods are much more potent for the SME than you probably would expect.*

*Two necessary conditions for maximizing outputs of a good marketing strategy are superior performance and competitive advantage.* We leave out much of the former in this book, as this is covered in large part by the futureSME project and manufacturing and service process improvements such as 'lean' that can help improve performance; *but what we do challenge here is the traditionally held notion that superior performance is simply a function of 'increased efficiencies'*. Superior performance is best achieved through effectiveness in delivering what the market actually needs; making what is actually needed and wanted rather than selling simply what we can make, leads to improved profitability and reduces wastage – ie lowering relative costs – and therefore also leads to greater, true, efficiencies. Reducing the emphasis and reliance on 'cost reductions' as the route to performance, and placing your emphasis and efforts on 'making to order/demand and need' through improving your responsiveness to the market, leads to genuine 'superior performance'. And makes it more sustainable.

Companies tend to have a resource-based view of strategy; we need to redefine this and see strategy as 'what we want to achieve' and tactics 'how we will achieve it', rather just 'applying what we have'. Strategy has to outline precisely what markets will be and how they will be served now and in the future, based on evidence from the market.

## Creating new markets

Every time we examine where we are, what market we are in, and how to improve our situation within a market, we are faced with the question: what can we do to find *more* customers and sales.

There is a paradox or conflict that exists between your current market and the new; your old customer and new; and overall 'what business are we actually in' and 'what business should we be in?'

We tend to see our markets as simply current and transient – those whom we currently serve with our core products that we know and love, being replaced by emerging new markets and needs that we see popping up almost every week with some accompanying new definition of the market and how we should supply to it. The time has come perhaps not to see markets as something we can define only in our terms, but understand that markets are now defining themselves and are ripe to be complemented by the new Competitive SME approach to aligning our proposition to meet their emerging new needs.

Lets take a look at Ansoff's matrix; this simple and effective illustration outlines the relative difference between where we are (current market with current products) through to where we would be if we make the biggest changes (new markets with new products). Although things are of course, a lot different when making those complex strategic decisions, Ansoff's matrix at least allows us to take a quick look on where and how we address the issue of 'creating new markets' for our propositions.

Before we start to look at the 'Ansoff dynamic' that precedes our investigation into expanding or changing our approach and strategic examination of our options, it *is a good time to reflect that most of our 'markets' are now being described and determined by others and not by ourselves*. Why is this distinction important? Because the fundamental change that we may set out on could begin entirely on the foundation of erroneous descriptions of our market, or the market into which we may be heading, as defined by others.

Put simply, if we are re-assessing the market or markets to get the most out of them and to improve our competitive position within them, WE NEED TO WORK WITH *OUR* DEFINITION OF IT. Apart from the obvious fact that defining our market is important in terms of accuracy – the existing one or in seeking a new one – it is also of note that this exercise should be undertaken only with an informed understanding of increasing risk. Not only in terms of preventing poor definitions, but also in fully considering the task that we will set ourselves, should we decide to move from our relative 'safe' position in simply serving the existing market with existing products (the first permutation in the matrix).

**FIGURE 5.2**   Ansoff's matrix

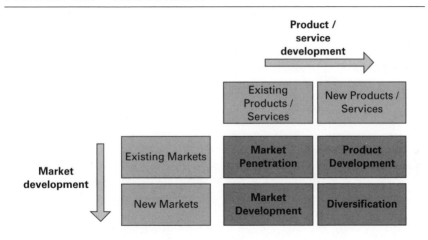

What I mean is that in seeking to move within the matrix, we have increased risks as we move from one permutation to another. The risk is not only in cost terms – indeed there normally is a price to pay in making any improvement or change – but that in moving to developing new products for our existing market, developing a different market for our existing products or in taking the major step of diversifying, the risk and costs can proportionately increase. So it pays to ensure that we not only make the right choice in terms of our strategy, but directly in ensuring that we involve the market and its precise definitions in our decisions when it comes to 'Ansoff's matrix'.

Typically, the risk is said to increase when we move in a 'Z' between the options. Moving from the first option, to the second, third and finally, the fourth and diversification. The issues of risk and cost are of course influenced by the way we define those options and indeed, in modern

**TABLE 5.1**   Making the right choice

| Option | SME issue | Comment |
| --- | --- | --- |
| **Market penetration** | • Increasing engagement and promotion<br>• Cut-throat and mature markets | • As long as the definition of the current market remains static<br>• Secure your customer base |
| **Product Development** | • SMEs are used to innovation<br>• Firmly establish core needs rather than relying on new functions or 'bells and whistles' | • See Product Development as a function of a greater understanding of the customer |
| **Market Development** | • May mean moving outside of your niche<br>• Needs significant 'market pull' | • Remember that a new 'market' may simply be based on an 'industry' rather than a common 'need'<br>• Needs the 'way to be paved' before it is entered |
| **Diversification** | • Always scary! | • Working from needs, backwards, makes this change less of an issue; especially if one understands needs better than the competitors and satisfy those needs to a greater degree |

marketing terms, the lines between the options may be more than a little blurred. Clearly in some cases, the old definitions may still exist; but where so much is changing, not least in how a 'product' or 'proposition' is structured and experienced, the SME should consider how the market would see any strategic change rather than simply the view from inside the organization.

Ansoff's matrix, whilst of some use, should be better placed alongside your SWOT analysis and considered towards the end of your marketing research activities, as markets are becoming 'too difficult to put in boxes'!

# Self-creating markets and the new reality

## Social networking and the 'power of pull'

If only life was so simple that all we had to do to create and manage products and markets was place our customers, consumers and prospects into our little matrices and spreadsheets. As the modern world becomes more complex, not only in terms of what the markets want or provide, the challenge of communicating and delivering to those markets with their plethora of new channels, contact and delivery points is now so vast that it is ever harder to keep up and consistently deliver in all manner of ways.

 *'In today's environment, hoarding knowledge ultimately erodes your power. If you know something very important, the way to get power is by actually sharing it'* (Joseph Badaracco).

'Ansoff's' and other traditional views of 'what our market is and how we define it' have changed, particularly with the advent of 'social' and self-creating markets.

Should we keep collating and putting our customers into little tables and matrices so that we can 'fire messages in a targeted fashion', or should we grasp the opportunity that the new connected and collaborative world of online communities and 'social' networks offer us as a means to engage?

The irony is that we now have a situation where even the most finite, 'nichest of niche' markets can come together by themselves, self-generating spontaneously to strategize, developing ideas, needs and products and forming comprehensive 'communities of interest' or clustering in and around supply chains; we are now facing the *most powerful and potent marketing channels of our time.*

 ## Social media communities

*Can we create communities that share interests and needs?* Can we control them so that they prefer our products and services to others? Most probably, we can do neither. This is arguably a good limitation; for if we tried to usurp or control this phenomenon (as many marketers have stated publicly they would wish to do) this really would be misunderstanding what is actually happening in the digital world of communities. We can however, engage with them. *Likewise, these new 'social' communities – both consumer and business communities – are a perfect fit with any new emphasis and activities in word-of-mouth marketing management and a terrific new opportunity for the SME to 'level the playing field' with larger organizations when it comes to successful positioning in the market.* (More on this subject in Chapter 7: Real market presence.) Of course, do not be put off creating your own social feed or presence that effectively *may* become a community or multi-way communication channel facilitated by you, which is something quite different from 'owning' it.

The advent of the new social networks and communities offers the SME unprecedented opportunities to refine strategic issues reflected in Ansoff's matrix and helps in turn lessen the risk associated with change to your developing products, services and 'markets'.

# Strategy and measurements for decision-making

The notion of strategy, as it relates to and binds marketing with overall company strategy and improves it, could be best represented in the Table 5.2; marketing gives the organization a new, virtuous and invigorated attitude to markets, change and improvement; changing and transforming our approach from an outdated 'inside out' perspective to one of 'outside in'.

Strategies, and many of their strategic marketing components and various activities, are increasingly best performed in *real time* – a modern necessity given the rate at which markets move and change dynamically and quickly. Neither the SME, nor its customers, has the time to take out of busy schedules to strategize...

Various measurements demonstrate a conflict between 'inside' and 'outside' our organization as described above. *These measurements provide a major hurdle in our quest to becoming more competitive.*

---

'Most measurements and metrics only tell us that we have a problem – they don't warn us beforehand or give us an insight into what we should do to prevent them!' (Regis McKenna).

---

Sales targets, production efficiencies, batch sizes, tasks, priorities, problems, 'solutions', stock levels, product development cycles/timing, etc clash throughout the supply chain, between the organization and its markets.

**TABLE 5.2**   Inside out v outside in

| 'Inside Out' view | 'Outside In' view |
|---|---|
| Plan ahead based on current market intelligence and know-how in meeting needs that may arise in the near future | Plan in real-time and address challenges, opportunities and changing needs as they occur |
| **Reactive**: be led by competition | **Proactive**: Sense & Respond |
| Resources focus | Opportunities focus |
| Legacy of skills and processes | Adaptability and Resilience |
| Structure of organization | Customer dynamics |
| Current / old market structure as defined by the industry | Changing structure of the market as defined by the customer |
| Work to our fullest capacity, making as much as we can | Maximize our impact on the market, and our value to it |
| **Make to margin and then *sell*** | **Make to need and to *order and demand*** |

© Copyright David James Hood: Competitive SME

Indeed, these measurements often clash within the organization! Many standard measurements used in business tend to underpin and intensify those conflicts and indeed may actually cause many of them. For example, it is best to be very, very wary of a strategy based on 'sales forecasts'.

*It is no longer acceptable, or indeed fruitful (if ever it was), to see all measurements and activities in isolation from each other; that is contra to a modern 'systems' and market or marketing based approach to competitive advantage. Indeed, these conflicts and 'fixation on the internals' are at the root of the organization's inability to be innovative, adaptive and 'customer centric'. The internal view of what is commonly understood as 'performance' is actually contrary to, and conflicts with, the external one.*

Measurements, as well as other matters that affect decision-making, cannot be taken in a vacuum and need deliberate input and alignment with the market. This obviously includes one of the most important measurements – or at least foremost presumption – that is involved in business: the basis of setting targets and making predictions for income generation.

Where is the money coming from? What will be the best proposition to bring to the market or adopt from our existing stable of products? What is our ideal customer or consumer? Where will they look for, or buy, our products and services? What pricing structures and points will ensure that we make not only good sales but also good profits, and help our market achieve their financial and non-financial aims too?

These and other decisions and predictions can only be based on market dynamics and an insight that results from real intelligence. Most measurements are usually way off the mark; most businesses measure: a) what they can; b) what they are told is what other organizations measure; c) what seems to be easy; d) without much care for the reality that is the dynamics and reality of the market. If everyone at the annual board meeting agrees to 'increase sales by 5 per cent year on year', this means nothing unless it has been evidenced that not only is this achievable, but why, where and how. And indeed if it can be 5 per cent or whether it should be another figure.

So let us think about this for a moment. What would give you greater confidence: knowing that your calculated and projected figures were as accurate as they could be at that time, or knowing that you are measuring the right things in the first place? This is not an easy matter to confront as, for example, establishing 'sales income figures' are a well-established prediction and measurement activity usually just because they are easily set and measured. The way that we do this needs addressing because unless we are doing really well and securing all the revenue we need (and didn't need to read this book!) *then our measurements are not working*. Our measurements are actually standing in the way of true innovation and true productivity. The scourge of true productivity and competitiveness lies with the next issue... one that is perhaps the greatest example of traditional, wrongful measurements that also leads to dreadful decision-making.

'Marketing should focus on market creation, not market sharing'.

(Regis McKenna)

#  Cost-plus and cost-accounting are the enemy of the SME

It is all right to try and be as 'lean and mean' as one can; but we SMEs have cut all the costs that we can, reducing our investments in important resources and activities that at some stage seemed quite necessary (and probably were!) and we are constantly on the treadmill of cutting costs. Cost-plus pricing and cost-accounting leads to an unhealthy and unending focus on costs, and this is reflected not only in our wrongful measurements and downward spiral, but in the way that we determine 'value'; it leads to wrongful determination of 'value' and setting erroneous 'pricing points' that we would charge others for our output. One of my learned marketing colleagues once said 'the most cost-effective, cost-focused and lean company is one that has ceased trading. Its costs have dropped down as far as it could go. What? Is that not what the accountant and finance director wanted?' *Reductions in cost for their own sake are not additive*; that is, costs saved in one place do not necessarily save the organization any money overall. Indeed, they may increase costs to the organization overall. Cost reduction activity is ironically the opposite of stability for the organization and has a definite limit – ZERO.

*We discussed at the outset of this book that being 'lean', by constantly cutting this and that, keeps us awake at night and worrying unduly.* It can lead to cutting service and the value we bring to the market. The opposite would, surprisingly, be a better approach; let us adopt a lean approach, being as efficient as we can, but in tandem with this we should resource up 'market-facing aspects' of the business, enabling us to 'listen more aggressively'. We need, in this age of modern marketing and multiple communications and markets, not only to be 'there'; we need to be 'out there', engaging and engaged.

'Cost-plus' and 'margin-based pricing' means that 'market pricing' and 'pricing by value' is unthinkable and unattainable. PERIOD.

We will come back to the issue of pricing later in the book.

# Purpose

It is more important to have a 'purpose' than simply a 'mission'. Some famous person once said something to that effect, and it is entirely true. Our mission could be to make some great products, excelling in a certain area, but we need to reflect on the purpose of why we are doing it in the first place. That keeps us focused on the goal – to make money and enable all of our stakeholders to reach their own goals. Likewise, any attempt at a 'purpose', 'mission statement' etc needs to ensure what we end up with is clear and it actually means something; it is not acceptable to simply get some good sounding words together as a statement that, when read, merely sounds glib, such as 'to be the highest quality provider of widgets in the western world'. We need to have high-level, aspirational and worthwhile statements strongly reflecting and complementing the developing USP and the 'brand' and meaning something powerful that resonates with prospects, customers and consumers in our markets.

## Decision-making and improving judgement

In making decisions, apart from obviously making the right ones, we also need to take cognizance of the most important decision – whether the decision that we are contending with at any time is *ACTUALLY ADDRESSING A PRIORITY REVENUE GENERATING ISSUE*. Specifically, in seeking to maintain and change our organization's financial health for the better, we desperately need to have a *cast-iron way to prioritize* any of the 'four I's' – Improvements, Investments, Innovations and Initiatives. It really does help to, rather than simply to list decisions, give them a priority; some may not be needed!

## Growth v growth

What do YOU consider 'growth' to be in terms of what you would want to achieve for your business? This is a similar old adage to the descriptions or aspirations for 'success'. I find 'growth' both irritating and indeed counterproductive as a term, and it usually results in an ill-judged strategy. I don't mind a manager or director wishing to 'grow sales' or something similar that leads us towards our goals. But I find that to 'grow market share' or grow the number of products in a range, customer numbers, market segments, prospect numbers, margins, company value or size and many other areas we are supposed to focus on 'growing' can actually prevent us from attaining the main goals – revenue and profit.

*Accountants and finance people (and others) have almost a 'Malthusian' view of business and markets: an assumption that all markets (or companies) grow with no limits to growth or transaction potential. The world is finite in size!*

> 'A "Malthusian" view exists: an assumption that all markets (or companies) grow with no limits to growth or transaction potential.'
>
> (Regis McKenna)

Exhausting your organization's resources prevents it from flourishing; so be careful of any objective for 'growth'. Focus on growing more time with the customer, freeing capacity to over-deliver and grow *value*.

# Do not neglect marketing when concentrating on sales!

In maximizing the management of an SME towards the goals of maintaining and improving revenue and profit, the fact of the matter is that greater alignment between sales and marketing leads to greater sales and business growth.

*Salespeople need marketers and managers responsible for marketing to:*

- listen to the market and align the whole proposition, production/delivery and marketing activities to it;
- add true value to the proposition, to make it easier to sell;
- ensure that the most effective and targeted messages (and two-way communications) are in place and undertaken to engage with the market;
- provide sales with good, essential leads and firm opportunities (and help them *prioritize* those opportunities);
- provide them with the correctly structured and warmed-up market (a market that knows the organization and its proposition, and within which the organization can have a distinctive profile and positioning);
- fill up the top of the 'sales funnel' and offer a satisfactory 'handover'.

*Marketing and managers responsible for marketing need sales and salespeople to:*

- listen out for the buzz and changing needs of the market (and properly 'formalize' that listening process and ensure sufficient time is given to that practice);
- add value to the proposition (their role is also a very substantive part of the proposition!);
- behave in a way that reflects a overriding concern for the well-being of the customer and less about figures and quarters (customers and consumers are people!);
- care about ongoing value and contact post-sale, *just as much as they did pre-sale*, perhaps even more;
- provide the company with closed sales;

- 'squeeze out' new customers and completed sales from the bottom of the 'sales funnel'.

*... However, do not split the funnel.* Marketing and sales – whether they are different departments, functions, people or activities – need to work together in tandem on 'the funnel'. Prospects and customers or consumers are not just 'hot items' to slickly pass on from marketing to sales.

 It would really help if we *stopped* using the two sets of figures shown in Figure 5.3.

**FIGURE 5.3**   Two sets of figures to stop using

Market Exposure & Number of Sales
(Prospects)    (Transactions)

A 'continuous' funnel is needed that works instead with a combination of marketing and sales efforts on a *REVENUE MACHINE rather than the sales cycle and that is quite different from the above transactional view*, resulting in common goals for both sales and marketing activities. (See more about the Revenue machine in Chapter 10 and changing sales to improve revenue)

Good quality of prospects or leads and performance directly increases sales productivity (by a large factor); word-of-mouth marketing working with word-of-mouth sales similarly helps align both activities, in turn fuelling the 'revenue cash machine'. Both of these activities and those involved in carrying them out *need to see engagement with the market as more than a single flow pipeline*; sales and marketing both need to work together on the customer experience and enjoyment and ensure that a *two-way pipeline and process* is working at all times. (For instance, let us get away from seeing 'customer service' as simply handling and reducing complaints after a sale and a necessary evil at best!)

 We need to move towards a 'dashboard' that is meaningful for the SME; we should measure only where it is important to measure, where we know we can maintain our business and revenue if we keep those metrics at an optimum; and that is achievable by using the *competitive marketing triangle* as your SME revenue dashboard. (We deal with the CMT later in Chapter 12.)

# Customer relationship management (CRM)

We do have to cover CRM in this book, for a number of good reasons. CRM has been painted as the panacea of managing data and creating and maintaining worthwhile relationships with the customer or consumer; it is however seen wrongly as merely the technology used within the customer-contact process. It is even accepted that CRM is – or gives us – the means to have some dashboard based on the market; that is both wrong and dangerous; to assume that data input into a CRM technology can determine the scope of what we need to provide and perform in terms of serving the market is unwise and misguided.

It is not just simply a case of heeding a warning against the old problem of 'garbage in, garbage out'. But with CRM, we can end up relying on incidental and transactional data that does nothing to give us a clearer picture of the needs of the market or how we should serve them, nor does it offer a priority or list of tasks to maintain and improve our revenue generating capability.

'Is there anything more impersonal or unfriendly than, "Please choose from the following eight options," followed by 10 minutes of hold music? Sadly, an automated telephone attendant, plus maybe an e-mail form on the Website, is all that connects most companies to their customers' (David Meerman Scott).

*CRM needs to:*

- Be seen strategically and operationally as a process, not a technology or information repository.
- Manage all the prospect, customer or consumer 'touch points'.
- Not just allow for the assessment and management of transactions, but build and maintain value.
- Realize new opportunities to use 'cloud' IT capabilities that make it easier to take and configure the systems that you need – rather than customizing or installing costly 'big-business monster systems'.
- Reflect that any CRM or customer management system needs to look after and nurture both the immediate customer in the chain and where it can, the *end* customer and consumer. And it allows for a 'social' component to deal with the new digital communications.

- Be leveraged properly alongside word-of-mouth measurement and management – otherwise 'CRM' will be nothing more than very subjective (and quickly out of date) opinion about people and companies rather than mirroring market realities.

# SME\ Incoming or 'in-bound' conversations

*(A very low cost way to increase your business, the SME's reputation and an overlooked, low-cost opportunity to engage with your market!)*

In addition to word-of-mouth marketing, inbound communications from your customer or consumer offer a major opportunity to nurture, keep, satisfy and 'delight' them. We have all experienced bad service when contacting a selling company; and conversely and strangely, we do not come across good 'contact handling' very often. When a customer or consumer gets in touch with you or your organization, whatever the reason, this should be seen as no less important than a sales opportunity. Indeed, it may of course be just that too; but it should be seen as a golden chance to do something much more:

- Use in-bound calls and correspondence effectively in conjunction with CRM.
- Make the customer or consumer feel important (by doing more than just telling them that they are important!).
- A major opportunity to resolve any issues and improve your product or service proposition.
- Can be used to reinforce your 'brand positioning'.
- Exploit a measurement that is both important and credible; you are getting feedback straight from the market and from someone *who is caring enough to open dialogue.*
- Invite them to do more than speak with you and resolve and issue or inform them; you can invite them into your 'virtual panel' of interested stakeholders (technologies are becoming available for this now).
- One in-bound contact 'episode' can lead to many months and years of a true 'relationship' with the individual or company making the approach.
- One in-bound conversation can lead to valuable WOM projection to that person or company's peer groups, colleagues, friends and networks ('viral' marketing).
- Do not make it difficult for the customer or consumer to get in touch; far too many people are 'guided' to faceless and indifferent

FAQ (frequently asked questions) lists buried within some websites or automatic answering system. What this says to your prospect, customer or consumer is 'we cannot be bothered speaking with you about anything; go away.' We can really do so much better and a lot can be gained in building competitive advantage by getting rid of those systems and policies and actually making an effort to *speak with those who are using their own valuable time to take the trouble to communicate with us.*

- Look at how people communicate and the patterns of contact; check your opening times, your call-receiving process, your complaint handling, make it clear what staff and colleagues will do when contacted and what it really means to the company. (This means more than telling them to give each caller only two minutes then ditch them, as many call centres are doing.) Don't have the customer or consumer doing too much – remove hurdles and have their concerns or enquiry handled effectively by people who have the power and ability to quickly make a difference to the customer or consumer.

- Follow up each contact with an appropriate summary direct to the contact by e-mail or postal correspondence; ensure that all is followed up, even if the issue is seen to be 'complete' as there is a natural tendency to move onto your next issue and forget to check.

- Put the individual on a long-term call-back plan, keep sending relevant and timely information sensitively, and contact them again later about their explicit issue of concern (this does not mean just sending more sales literature and penalizing them for getting in touch).
  Work wholly within data protection legislation and recognized codes of practice; make sure that individuals only get the kind of information they wish, when they wish it and in the correct way with full permission granted.

- Ensure that all your outgoing messages include the invitation to converse with your people.

- Don't replace people with technologies just because you can and you think it will cut costs and 'hassle'; *technology should be used only when it removes a major constraint in the business that results in more money, convenience and rewards for your customer or consumer – and for constraints that a person cannot handle.*

- Elevate and reinforce the belief that speaking with a customer or consumer is the most important activity in your organization and that conversation is key to everyone's ongoing prosperity.

- Use a word-of-mouth measurement system to maximize your return on investment in managing incoming conversations; ask prospects and customers to contact you and then ask again! (See final pages in Chapter 12 about WOM marketing and management.)

It is very strange that we spend SO much money looking for customers and consumers, hopefully and subsequently turning them from prospects into paying us some attention... then all but IGNORING incoming opportunities to have meaningful discussions with the market once we have found them.

*Let us change that right now.*

"*People expect good service but few are willing to give it.*

**ROBERT GATELY**

**FIGURE 5.4**   Chapter 5 summary action table

| ☑ | **CHAPTER 5 Summary Action Table** |
|---|---|
| ☐ | Determine and define what you would judge to be a 'success' for you and your organization |
| ☐ | What targets are there for making money? (Think about the needs of both the market and your organization rather than 'share of market', 'number of units' or 'number of transactions') |
| ☐ | Test the 'make to stock' v 'make to order' assumptions. (Note that you may of course need to make to stock; as it is required in many sectors. The objective is to break this conflict) |
| ☐ | Check where you are and could or should be on the Ansoffs Matrix; does your marketing intelligence give you an insight into where you would go from here? |
| ☐ | Proportion a ratio to the 'inside>out' and 'outside>in' views; for each line do you lean more towards one column or the other? Discuss with your key people |
| ☐ | Discuss how you set about constructing a price; who does it and why? How much is the market considered in this and how? Could it be improved? |
| ☐ | Have a go, with your Team, at defining your Purpose; don't worry if it isn't robust as you can revisit it later |
| ☐ | Get your sales and marketing people (and agents if you use them) around the table to see how both 'functions' can help the other. Go through the 'salespeople need' and 'marketing needs' to prompt discussion and a healthy debate |
| ☐ | Offer a workshop to your customer-facing people who speak with the customer. 'How could we improve our listening and responding behaviour and processes?' |

**FIGURE 5.5**    Summary of the essentials from this chapter

competitive SME™

| What to CHANGE | | What to change TO | | HOW to change |
|---|---|---|---|---|
| | → | | → | |

**What to CHANGE**

- Unclear definition of 'success' as it relates to our SME
- How we currently use measurements and metrics
- Inside-out view
- Focus on cost reductions
- Obsessing about following 'new markets'
- Competing on low price
- Setting price as a cost-plus margin calculation
- Sales as a singular exclusive process
- Loose CRM activity
- Placing and keeping the customer at 'arms length'

**What to change TO**

- Clear goals and objectives
- We are driving rather than simply following the market
- Create a 'make to order' organization
- Outside-in view
- Value improvement
- Serve existing customers better and understand their needs more clearly
- Compete on more than just price (more later!)
- Use true market-based pricing
- Sales as a constant process
- Tighten CRM as a valuable process
- Invite them in!

**HOW to change**

- Focus on making decisions that matter
- Build the right product and service from the outset
- Align our interests with those of the market and use new measurements to gauge and support this
- Sense and Respond process that builds upon CRM
- Use market and needs based pricing; stop cutting everywhere and anywhere
- Balance existing v new markets
- Create a meaningful competitive advantage
- Look to generate income rather than 'transaction instances'
- Align sales & marketing to objectives and income rather than prospect building
- Widen sales people's role to include service
- Add all contact 'touch' points to the CRM system
- 'Morph' customer service and contact points into places to invite and respond

# Your unique selling proposition

## Agility, the 'adaptive organization', profit and revenue improvement

> *Feeling unique is no indication of uniqueness.* **DOUG COUPLAND**

Creating, refining and improving a unique selling proposition (USP) is not easy; ensuring that you have both a definitive and lasting USP is not without its additional challenges. That said, there is much you can do quickly, immediately and at relatively little cost. Ask yourself the following:

- How often do we try to deliver a consignment or act on a necessary action on behalf of the customer before the due date or when they expect something to be done?

- Do we make sure that the prospect or customer gets a call back as quickly as possible or when they wanted it?

- Have we recently called them to see whether our product or service was delivered and enjoyed satisfactorily and were they pleased with what they received and used the product/service to best effect, thereby ensuring that they received the benefits they sought?

You may think that these questions do not relate to the subject of determining and developing your USP. What I simply wished to demonstrate here is that these are three examples that can readily be performed by companies and, more often than not, are not even considered. We often look for the difficult-to-find 'advantages' rather than the simple, never mind actually finding the definitive USP. We overlook the obvious and ignore the virtue in examining what can be done readily.

What has to be remembered is that despite our primary role as creators and providers of products and services, each and every SME is now a 'service on demand' company. Consumers and business buyers all have higher expectations that *we should be excellent at customer service and constantly on-demand*... and if we do not even do the simple checks and often quite effortless tasks to keep them happy, then we will not stand a chance against the competition. It is not about the customers' loyalty and attention they would give to us, it is about our loyalty and attention we consistently give to them. (This is a major fault with so-called loyalty schemes beloved by retail chains and consumer goods providers.)

Projecting our USP is not about stating to our markets, at every possible opportunity, that we have 'skills and capabilities'; it is about *demonstrating those caring skills and capabilities, at every opportunity that we have to do so*, especially when the customer needs to pull those services 'on-demand' or when they least expect to see or hear from us. Adding a good degree of refined and valued service to your product is not about just ensuring conformance to a standard level or to some 'SLA' (service level agreement); it is a fantastic opportunity to give *more* than was expected, at no or low cost. Nevertheless, it can be highly valued. *That is when you truly deliver a USP. A USP is only such when it is delivered, valued and truly unique.*

## Advantage and 'the product'

We now live in a world where an advantage is rarely related principally to the actual, physical, product; it is very often an added component, a specific critical feature or bolt-on service or other proposition element that is most valued by the individual customer and is key to success. Just as 'knowledge is power', your 'intellectual assets' are not only limited to the physical difference your product may have, but to the perceptions and intangible elements that surround it. This is a critical area for SMEs to grasp and grapple with; it is ultimately not only where the immediate USP lies but where the future worth and value of the company will be maintained and protected.

'A high degree of complacency intensified by a cost focus results in an increasing degree of commoditization; however a high degree of engagement and giving more to the customer succeeds in creating greater differentiation...'

Digressing here slightly, let us take a few moments to think about EQUITY. We know that shareholders or owners of an organization – you may be in that position – constantly think about the share of the organization in which they have an ownership stake. It is readily (but not accurately!) converted into monetary value. *However, other forms of 'equity' such as 'customer equity' or 'brand equity' are less often considered by the SME – and the SME can benefit markedly by seeing both its customers and brands as something to be nurtured as assets in their own right, as opposed to simply a conduit to money.*

## Resourcing to create advantage

Related to the issue of exceptional added-value customer service is the issue of capacity. We always think that we need a lot more people and resources to create and make our products and services, and less to actually ensure their correct and optimal delivery.

That may sometimes be the case, but we should ensure that not only do we have adequate resources allocated to proper pre and post-sale service, we should ensure that we do indeed have *excess resource capacity* overall. (Incidentally, as suggested earlier, that after-sales service, truly and meaningfully deployed is an exceptional – and quite unique – way to grow word of mouth up at the 'recommend wholeheartedly' end of the WOM scale; the customer is more likely to stick with you through good times and bad and more likely to become happily involved in product or proposition development activities. After-sales and ongoing service should also be developed whilst physically sitting WITH the customer after the sale where possible.)

Why should we try to free up these resources? *Because we always need some extra capacity.* Life has a funny way of continually throwing up major challenges when we least expect them, and for an SME this can be critical. When we get hit by a major unexpected trauma – such as a problem with an order or a customer that is unsatisfied – this can lead to huge repercussions to both our profitability and our 'perceived value and trustworthiness' in the market. That is why we need 'excess capacity storm troopers' to react quickly to any and every customer or prospect's call for help.

 Remember, to be successful, you do not have to have every resource working at full capacity; you know this to be intuitive yet we all surrender to received thinking that everyone and everything has to be working 100 per cent of the time. This is counterproductive and a hurdle to agility, competitiveness and incompatible with the wish to focus.

As well as forever striving to work to capacity, another enemy of profit lies in our way: we need to battle the inevitable, almost gravitational, pull towards doing less for our market. We strive to cut costs where we can and to increase margin (that often means cutting costs by reducing the available margin to everyone else!) and *we end up wanting to do less for the customer, not more.* Our whole being wishes that we could do less, but the customer or consumer wants more and more.

That gravitational pull perversely makes us inherently commoditize our product (see *The Marketing Manifesto* book for more on this subject); and commoditizing our product is precisely what we DO NOT WANT. So what can we do to counter this commoditization, to increase competitiveness and differentiate ourselves, and perhaps even make ourselves immune to commoditization?

That equation is simple; is the authentic line of attack to competitiveness as simple?

# SWOT analysis

An essential and traditional tool used within marketing and business strategy is the SWOT analysis. It allows for an assessment of 'where we are' and is useful as a strategic tool and one to help facilitate discussions about some long-held or developing assumptions and to challenge them. It is a terrific and simple tool to start the strategic planning and marketing planning activity as it helps us define 'what is the over-arching problem?' It helps us construct a picture of the high-level problem and the reverse – the immediate and aspirational goals and objectives we would like for the business.

There are some variations of this simple tool, but the essential four components are:

## Strengths

What do you – and more importantly your market – think are your real core competencies and key ingredients that separate you out from the rest? Where are the obvious cash generators in your business and what is the genuine 'story' that best describes to others why they should buy from you?

## Weaknesses

Is there any major problem, in terms of our ability to sense and respond to the market, which is standing in our way of improving our capabilities to serve it? Are there any major constraints internally that we need to unblock?

## Opportunities

We know that there are always opportunities for us as an organization; do we know what they actually are, are we able to prioritize them; can we list them in order of their likelihood to generate money and are they realistic?

Are there any constraints within the market that we could alleviate or unblock? Are there any foremost needs or wants that we can fulfil, perhaps better than others?

## *Threats*

Do we fully realize what threats exist, where they come from and what form they will take? Threats do not always come from an obvious competitor activity invading your territory; they come from any of the 'forces in the marketplace' and from the unlikeliest places!

There are a few maxims often associated with the SWOT analysis that do need to be challenged: that if you have a strength, then it cannot be a weakness and vice versa; likewise an opportunity cannot at the same time pose a threat. It is also said that strengths and weaknesses come from within the company, and opportunities and threats are external issues. It may help to reflect on those maxims to some extent; the SWOT table and analysis is a great tool to start some really insightful debate within an SME.

 There is however, a danger and perhaps natural inclination to go straight into the SWOT analysis without taking some well-defined steps before it is attempted.

Moreover, there may be an inclination to do it alone; SWOTs should be undertaken with as many key stakeholders as possible within and outside of the company, where appropriate. This inclination is probably due to the fact that is seems a somewhat simple exercise, and indeed it is only usually demonstrated as 'four small boxes in a 2×2 table'.

We also may think that we can answer all the questions posed by SWOT using our existing knowledge; this of course misses the main opportunity to undertake what can be a powerful but simple and quick review of our current business position. It can also have the added disadvantage that it will generate a huge list of items within each criterion; however, we need to resist simply making too long and unprioritized or unweighted lists and try and focus by ruthlessly prioritizing the SWOT short lists that we create. This activity can also lead to offering more discussion and clarification, rather than just an assessment, and offering a glimpse of possible options for a way forward.

The SWOT analysis should not be used alone or in isolation from the marketplace and its reality. It should be used in a collective and inclusive fashion, in that any of the component points reflect aggregates, not specific people or individual gripes or spurious ideas. We are dealing with many subjective issues when performing SWOT analyses, and it pays to ensure that we get whatever evidence we can, at the outset. Remember that the usual rules apply for SWOT as for 'brainstorming' to ensure that clear objectives are to be the result, no subject is off limits, no ideas or perceptions of any of the four components are invalid and all must be checked with the market at some point – the earlier the better!

*Table 6.1 provides an updated and amended SWOT table to make it considerably more effective for the SME.* (This can be used in conjunction with an assessment of 'Porters Five Forces' in the next chapter.)

**TABLE 6.1**    SWOT analysis

| STRENGTHS | WEAKNESSES |
|---|---|
| The good things we do well and the major aptitudes we have as an organization | The things we don't do well and where we could improve; internal obstacles and constraints that prevent us reaching our goal |
| New improvement | New improvement |
| • Realize that our strengths are not always what we think or tell ourselves that they are<br>• Understand that 'strengths' as we see them may be markedly different from any the market may list | • They are often described as 'underutilized strengths'; this is a misnomer and misleading and will result in us dealing with issues that may not be important or are a lesser priority |
| **OPPORTUNITIES** | **THREATS** |
| The changes and vagaries of the market that present us with new options; constraints that can be alleviated or removed that are external to our organization and exist in the market | What forces within the market and elsewhere that exist or could exist adversely affect the health and efficacy of our organization and our attractiveness to the market |
| New improvement | New improvement |
| • Assess possible opportunities as rapidly as possible and rule in or out quickly<br>• Refocus our attention on constraints<br>• See ourselves as valuable sources of opportunities for change from within<br>• Test and qualify any opportunities using Perceptual Maps | • Move our focus away from an addiction to competitor analyses as the major focus for competitive reaction and tactics, and turn our focus instead toward those real and specific threats |

'*Even for the SME, your brand is arguably your most important asset; it stores and projects your worth, integrity, your value to the market, your people, your whole proposition; it also encompasses, exploits and protects that hard-won and valuable intellectual property. It protects you.*'

When conducting a SWOT analysis, it is useful to consider whether your current intellectual components of the 'proposition' and organization's capabilities that constitute 'valuable knowledge' are indeed valuable assets. 'Intellectual assets' as a term is probably well understood by SMEs involved in technically advanced manufacturing in terms of protectable technology and technical advantages – such as patents – but what is less recognized or understood is that the branding and intangible elements described earlier, the perceptions the market has of your organization, the people you have, the company structures, procedures, processes, combined 'smarts' – 'how things are done here' – *all can be forms of your organization's intellectual power and value.*

## It is a knowledge economy now!

**FIGURE 6.1**    The three components of intellectual policy

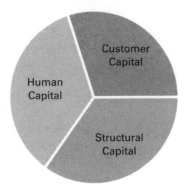

*In creating our competitive advantage, we need to take cognizance of how that advantage can be considered a valuable ASSET, not just heighten an immediate tactic.* SME owners and managers know that for many years, we have been competing within what is now known as 'the knowledge

economy' where it is strategically important for organizations to identify, nurture, grow and protect their 'smarts'.

Thomas A Stewart has published some exceptional works on the subject of examining and fostering the creation and management of intellectual capital within organizations; these books are a must-read for the SME. He differentiates between the 'assets' that are *human capital, customer capital* and *structural capital*. (See Table 6.2 below for some helpful descriptions.)

**TABLE 6.2**   Intellectual assets table

| Intellectual Asset | Description and Opportunity |
| --- | --- |
| **Human Capital**<br><br>*(PEOPLE!)*<br><br><br>• *Who knows what?*<br>• *What latent specialisms exist?*<br>• *Is there a 'Capability' Register for everyone's skills?*<br>• *Can we 'centralize' knowledge?* | • This is the knowledge residing in the heads of your people<br>• It is said that people are the #1 asset of any organization; yet they are rarely treated as such or nurture accordingly<br>• If you can tap into it, it provides a source of competitive advantage<br>• **There is an opportunity to 'codify' this asset as most of it will otherwise remain inside their brains rather than be committed to a central repository or somewhere it can be reproduced and exploited by the whole organization** |
| **Structural Capital**<br><br>*(COMPANY)*<br><br><br>• *How do we do things around here?*<br>• *What processes are peculiar to us?*<br>• *What I.P. is ours, what is protectable?* | • This is the tangible intellectual property or 'easily articulated' elements of our company that is transcribed into patents, technical advantages and regular 'property'<br>• **The opportunity exists to capture both Human Capital and Customer Capital and change it into Structural Capital that can be better protected and harnessed if codified** |

**TABLE 6.2** *continued*

| Intellectual Asset | Description and Opportunity |
|---|---|
| **Customer Capital**<br><br>*(MARKET)*<br><br><br>• *Do we know our best customers?*<br>• *Who can form our panels?*<br>• *Whom can we trust to give honest, good feedback?*<br>• *What value has our brand in the market?* | • This is the value created and maintained by the relationships and WOM management in the market<br>• Marketing is said to be worth 3 times more to the organization than other 'functions'; this is because of its understanding of the market<br>• **The opportunity exists to manage WOM and build the 'brand value' of the organization and its proposition in the market; thus resisting price commoditization and increasing the opportunity for a 'good price'** |

© Copyright David James Hood: Competitive SME

It is extremely worthwhile to audit, log and maintain a register of intellectual assets for all types of 'accrued capital' and treat them as items that require constant and consistent nourishment, ongoing investment and consistent protective vigilance.

A useful intellectual asset check is easy to produce on a simple spreadsheet to help you identify and begin a very worthwhile new approach to managing value for your organization.

Moreover, remember to include your BRANDING and any intangible elements in your register, to be both protected and nurtured!

**FIGURE 6.2**   Chapter 6 summary action table

| ☑ | CHAPTER 6 Summary Action Table |
|---|---|
| ☐ | How often do we consider and act on all elements of delivery – above what is expected? Where can we do more? (Do a workshop with your key people) |
| ☐ | When we improve, do we actually free up resources or just cut them accordingly? Can we free up some people's time – not to just do something else, but regroup and consider some of the above ideas? |
| ☐ | Can we create a repository to Log, Nurture and Maintain our I.P. (spreadsheet, database etc.)? |
| ☐ | Identify where, and with whom, our I.P. lies. Do an I.P. Audit |
| ☐ | Do a SWOT Analysis as an internal workshop |

© Copyright David James Hood: Competitive SME

**FIGURE 6.3**　Summary of the essentials from this chapter

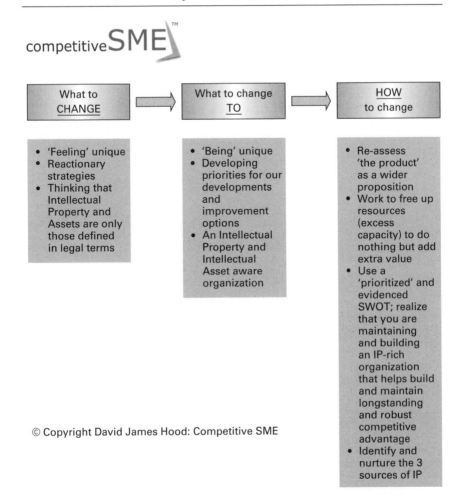

competitive SME™

| What to CHANGE | What to change TO | HOW to change |
|---|---|---|
| • 'Feeling' unique<br>• Reactionary strategies<br>• Thinking that Intellectual Property and Assets are only those defined in legal terms | • 'Being' unique<br>• Developing priorities for our developments and improvement options<br>• An Intellectual Property and Intellectual Asset aware organization | • Re-assess 'the product' as a wider proposition<br>• Work to free up resources (excess capacity) to do nothing but add extra value<br>• Use a 'prioritized' and evidenced SWOT; realize that you are maintaining and building an IP-rich organization that helps build and maintain longstanding and robust competitive advantage<br>• Identify and nurture the 3 sources of IP |

© Copyright David James Hood: Competitive SME

*The only sustainable competitive advantage is the ability to learn faster than the competition.*

ARIE DE GEUS

# Real market presence

## Marketing on a budget; branding, positioning and the SME

> *O would some power the giftie gie us to see ourselves as others see us.* **ROBERT BURNS**

**A**n elegant way to influence demand – and one that is often overlooked by the SME – is to see further down your supply chain and take action there. Large companies understand this; this is why they spend vast sums of money convincing the end user to buy from their channel partners. That way, you can cover both fundamental bases: your immediate customer in the chain and your end user. How can this be done? Using the best and most cost-effective (and inexpensive) method: WORD OF MOUTH. *And it is more 'do-able' now than ever.*

> *Word of Mouth management 1: Customer = PUSH*
> *Word of Mouth management 2: Consumer = PULL*

Whether you provide to the business-to-business (B2B) or business to government or public sector (B2G/B2P) market – to a customer in your supply chain, or to the B2C market and its consumers – you can use WOM to manage both. It does of course require some time and effort; the whole point is that WOM as a managed activity is wholly focused on influencing WOM in the market and thus does need a degree of real effort. It cannot be a passive nor occasional pastime. But what you can get in return is well worth any continued effort you put in to this activity.

Effectively, many SMEs and other organizations 'push' their products into the chain, and leave the other 'downstream' organizations to sell and 'pull' from you and other suppliers. SMEs can forget about the final consumer – but so does your immediate customer! You can really reinvigorate your sales by adopting 'pull' with the end-user/consumer as well as improving 'push' to your customers.

That said, SMEs often shy away from the second word-of-mouth management opportunity; they understandably consider the consumer to be the realm of their channel partner 'downstream'. However, your channel partners will likely have their own agenda, their own range of product propositions to sell, and you could be very much at their mercy. I have seen this problem with a well-known high-street retailer that simply has a markedly different agenda than its manufacturing feeder companies – and the latter's health and longevity are not even on their agenda. It is not the SME's fault though; very few organizations really understand or have bothered to 'codify' how WOM could actually be used as a commercial tool! Certainly the business professions have not offered any leadership or grasped this most profitable of activities.

*At long last, IT IS TIME TO GRASP WORD OF MOUTH as a tool and the prime metric that determines the 'health' of our SME.*

Leave 'big-branded, heavy advertising campaigns' to big corporates that can afford such indiscriminate promotions; the SME should grasp WOM as THE main tool to create, maintain and improve revenue. Every opportunity to speak with any stakeholder – not just customers – should be used as an opportunity to gauge and influence word-of-mouth.

> **SME** *'Remember that word of mouth reaches into, works within, and can be very effective inside your own company too.'*

*You can, even with limited budgets, help create a BUZZ.* Think of any buzz surrounding a product that you know of; it does not even have to be a physical one; for instance a new movie can be made now with limited budgets, have a great hook or proposition (or indeed an innovative message or means of 'viral' delivery) and can be very successful indeed thanks to active WOM management. You can help the retail or 'downstream' part of your supply chain by helping create and sustain that buzz – with only a small amount of effort and investment in 'putting out a viral message' and managing WOM – using social marketing for instance. Likewise, you can sign up potential customers or consumers for trials that can subsequently be delivered by your channel partners – giving them more good prospects and helping them to help you. That way, you are becoming an indelible and critical source of knowledge and informed opinion; this goes a long way to developing and maintaining trust in you by your immediate customer.

As you build WOM and knowledge of *their* market – your ultimate market – they will offer you preferential trading terms and conditions and make you more of a priority. They will also likely value your relationship and brand over others.

Strangely, as modern business has placed hurdles between the producer and the customer or end-user/consumer (eg complex supply 'chains', letters instead of face to face, and now information technology and digital channels etc) this flies in the face of a good opportunity to develop relationships and WOM as a major tool for marketing. That is a real opportunity for the improvement-hungry and focused SME.

## Power and your market

Michael Porter stated that your market consists of five competitive forces that affect the 'power' within it. This point of view has been around for some time, still resonates today and it would be useful to consider it before planning and addressing your market and allied research and campaigning activities. In determining those *'power fault lines'*, you can prepare to shape your plan and activities to deal with those forces and act accordingly.

Porter's model is particularly useful when coupled with a SWOT analysis, product life cycle and alongside the other marketing tools contained in this book.

The 'five forces' model remains a potent tool in examining (and reminding us of the importance of) the market our organization inhabits – the so-called 'business ecosystem'.

Porter's five forces are illustrated and adapted slightly for Competitive SME in Figure 7.1.

What we need to do now in the 21st century is to examine those respective forces anew and, rather than having an unhealthy outlook on competition (as I have indicated by adding 'UNHEALTHY FOCUS' to the centre component 'Industry rivalry'), turn our talents to more productive activities by:

- partnering and securing suppliers;
- reducing the threat of substitutes;
- expelling potential entrants before they get in, or reducing their effect on your customers and market if they do;
- ... all by skewing the model and emphasis in favour of 'buyer power', meeting it head-on and being seen to do so.

**FIGURE 7.1** Porter's five competitive market forces

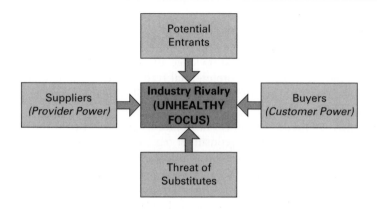

'WOM can eliminate the threats of entrants and substitutes, put stressful and distracting industry rivalry behind you and preserve your organisation's status as a preferred customer to your suppliers and a preferred supplier to your customers!'

To better manage and formally and comprehensively use this model to best effect, you can gauge how well you are addressing these five forces and coupling WOM with a new customer focus, and *adjusting the power towards the relationship 'boundary' between YOU and your customer.* We can measure what we wish to measure in our market as it is depicted above – size, money, numbers, products, share of market, 'participating organizations and individuals', offers, channels, etc etc – but most of these measurements are relative and not really helpful when it comes to making ourselves and our propositions more valuable and profitable – but WOM is most certainly a LOT more relevant and productive as a manageable and relevant metric.

*You can't do much to address three or four of the forces, but you can positively affect and exploit the customer force.*

Managed correctly, WOM can eliminate the threats of entrants and substitutes, put stressful and distracting industry rivalry behind you and preserve your organization's status as a preferred customer to your suppliers and a preferred supplier to your customers!

# Assessing your market: marketing and market research

An essential and standard prerequisite for good marketing, sales and any commercial activity is of course comprehensive market or marketing research. The difference between the two is the subject of many debates, but essentially *market research* is wider – it is the exploratory activity undertaken at a 'helicopter' level to examine whether there is a market, whether it is worth exploring further and entering into it, as a 'sector' or 'segment'. *Marketing research* is altogether more specific, focusing on an existing market, marketing 'mix' and proposition and working out how to better address the market with a change to your proposition.

In either case, doing your homework at the earliest stage results in better marketing and the chance of subsequent success. As an SME, we have not just to ensure that any research we undertake is cost effective but we have to ensure that it is relevant, incisive and must be pertinent to our strategic or tactical options as they relate to our specific circumstances and context. Far too many off-the-shelf 'research or industry reports' are too generic and talk about industry averages that don't exist (as no company is an 'average' and each company, even in the same sector or industry, is quite different in terms of its strategy, its products, its customers and many other operational variables!).

Your research has to be undertaken directly by you or your agents, based on specific criteria around the challenges and opportunities that exist for you and your company only. It is of course *YOUR* market or markets that you wish to explore or improve.

A simple 'research template' is offered below; the KISS (keep it simple) principle applies here; the most important input as ever, into any research is of course feedback and word of mouth, so don't forget to include the 'customer's voice' in your research and the options it reveals to you when the activity is completed.

 ## Market/marketing research template

1  *Goal for the research*: whether it is market or marketing research, to test, a change to be considered or already performed, perceptions, brand, recall/knowledge, new product or service development options etc.

2  *Background*: why there is a need for the research, its objectives (you are writing this for yourself and colleagues as a *working* document, not just to 'publish' or sit on a shelf!).

3 *Financial objectives*: what the output of the research will be used for, how much needs to be invested (in time as well as money) and what it must earn the organization in turn.

4 *Measurements*: how you are tying up this research with word-of-mouth metrics and your ongoing sensing using WOM (and if you haven't yet started a WOM sensing and management system now would be a great time to construct a rudimentary one – see Chapter 12 for measuring through WOM).

5 *Methodology*: how we are going to conduct our research, the sources we will use and any research activities we need to organize and resource to make it all happen; this includes how we will 'sense and respond' to customer input and capture and collate word of mouth feedback.

6 *Major findings*: of course, this section will be completed at the end of the project, or indeed, as it should, be updated when the research is revisited at a later time.

7 *Segments and targets*: this section deals with the type of customer or consumer markets sought or secured; using demographics or, more likely, some business profiles based on your 'value proposition' (see later) and who would benefit the most from your proposition.

'Consumption is the sole end and purpose of all production; and the interest of the producer ought to be attended to only so far as it may be necessary for promoting that of the consumer.'

8 *Engagement programme*: an expansion of the earlier section on methodology; this time covering in depth how you will work with your prospects and customers that may have indicated a desire or agreed to a more involved study. Can you spend time at your prospects' or customers' premises shadowing them and scrutinizing their day-to-day habits that affect your proposition development? (Can you witness and monitor your customer and consumer actually using the product or service – or variable to be tested – at point of delivery or use?)

9 *Key benefits analysis*: this includes some exploratory or refinement activities to check and test your key proposition elements (marketing mix) with your target market(s). You would map their needs here.

10  *State what you are going to do with the resulting information*: ie place it into SWOT analysis, feed it into new product development processes; review product life cycle; test/review/update perceptual plans, recommended changes to product or service, test and optimize the proposition and mix further, etc.

## Sources of information

In addition to more obvious resources, some of your best sources of information for research purposes are often overlooked:

- Those who have complained: they could even come back and buy again if you have demonstrated concern by contacting them afterwards for their input; indeed they will probably give their input readily.
- Libraries and librarians: they are well qualified – probably more so than ourselves – to research and 'retrieve information'; so even with the advent of the internet the value of professional researchers and 'retrievers' is high and very often low cost or indeed free.
- Professional trade or membership organizations and other groups and 'communities of interest' (with the above caveat and 'health warning' that these sources tend to be generic, and reports can be very insular, subjective and 'about the industry, not the customers or their needs').

## The 'value proposition'

(See also Chapter 10 on developing the value proposition as part of the sales and pricing process.)

A lot has been said and written under the term 'value proposition'. It is clear that much simply reflects an internal focus and definition of 'value' and 'proposition'; it usually means: 'Let us look at what we are good at, our core competencies, so that we can find some USP that will resonate with anyone.' These are not bad sentiments, but wholly inadequate to sustain a competitive advantage that would both be meaningful to the market and make money.

As stated earlier in this book, 'getting the proposition right' is directly proportional to reducing stress (for you and the business), getting more returns for efforts everywhere in the business, achieving a higher return on sales and marketing efforts, improving branding, cementing your position within the market, and gaining REAL productivity. *Can you therefore state your value proposition, in around 10 words?*

Likewise, how would you describe your competitors' propositions? Can you do that in 10 words? If you can do that for them, you can do it for yourself. (We will come back to that issue later.)

You can also check variations on those messages and statements; there is software available and methods to check variables. Look at how very sophisticated (but not always difficult to use) software systems can check varying keywords used in online adverts (click through rates analysed after running different adverts with different two variables, known as AB testing). Thanks to the power of computing both on the desktop and online, we can now start to play with and modify our messages and propositions to optimize the value proposition and how we convey it.

 Business is the science of the experiment; indeed, it is a perpetual series of experiments. Every result is positive, for any campaign or proposition test; even those that do not come up with the result you may have wished for. (For more ongoing information on software and technology that can help check and optimize your evidenced proposition in the market, see *The Epsilon project* for more on this in the Resources pages).

If any result is indeed 'negative' in that you didn't get the resulting action or improvement to your revenue that you predicted, remember that you found out how NOT to spend your money or make a change; you therefore know what didn't work – so are closer to knowing what will, and this is very much a positive. That said, the hard work still needs to be done. We still need to work out what will make us competitive, to find that true need, before we begin to look at moving forward and refining the proposition or testing what and how we would communicate the proposition and its USP to the market. We need to check out more of the 'marketing mix' elements before we can refine the message.

##  Have you fully clarified the value proposition?

A key approach used in classical modern marketing is to look at the 'layers' of a proposition – to understand what it is that we are actually offering – right from the essential and base core product, through to the whole proposition; *from the tangible to the intangible*. What we will look at now is the *total product concept* and the *value matrix*. Whilst doing so, we should always be aware of the dynamic tension between what *WE* see as the product, proposition and its associated value contrasted with what the *MARKET* would see and describe as 'value' and what it would value.

## The total product concept

Figure 7.2 gives a simple and well-understood illustration that is useful and quickly helps us determine and evaluate what it is that we provide. It helps us map out our existing, mainly tangible, product and the various 'layers' that we build upon it to form the entire proposition.

It also keeps track on developments in the market in terms of existing product/service and ongoing changes in the make up of the 'Ps' in the market and the level of sophistication and expectation within it.

**FIGURE 7.2**    The total product concept – original

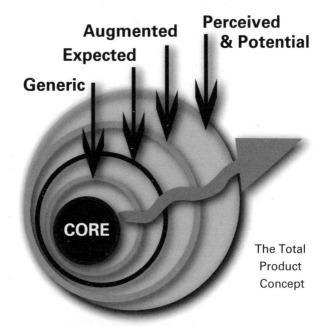

© Copyright David James Hood: Competitive SME

- *Core*: the 'tangible' part of the product or delivered utility; it is the physical article or pared-back item that you are offering. This could be said to describe the basic function of the product or proposition.
- *Generic*: the 'industry standard'; the description of the basic level of collected functions that defines the product category as understood by the market; it traditionally describes the market or industry segment that your organization inhabits.

- *Expected*: any market now demands more than just mere core or generic product features but has an embedded anticipation of enhanced benefits; the market needs and indeed wants more since it knows it can get it. This layer is increasingly demanding and expanding as the market expects more and more, as the core product correspondingly becomes less and less viable and competitive. (Hence, all the activities, discussion and debate about 'value add' and the need to see your product in terms other than what it physically embodies are vitally important to the SME). As the market demands more, the product becomes closer to a mere commodity.

- *Augmented*: these are usually the 'features, bells and whistles' we add, to enhance the product over and above what the market is used to. We strive to tweak with the expected product, to try and differentiate ourselves in the market and add what 'value' we can. *It is an increasingly valid and fruitful endeavour to debate and determine where the market currently is, and will be, between the 'expected' and the 'augmented' layers of your proposition on an ongoing basis.* This can help to determine whether your 'difference' is of value compared to what is out in the marketplace, whether you really have any virtuous differences and how close your products are to becoming 'standard' as opposed to 'exciting'! As the 'expected' layer inflates, the augmented layer compensates and the contest to add more and more, to innovate and add incremental improvements or service components dominates as competition intensifies.

- *Perceived/potential*: human perceptions, and the need to recognize them and their meaning as it relates to revenue potential and your position in the market, relate directly to your ability to compete; this layer again reflects and affects the dynamic the dynamic tension between the various layers and where key elements of the 'value proposition' can be attained. This layer should far exceed the augmented layer and it is obvious that the more you are (well) perceived, the greater the likelihood for success in the market due to the establishment of a highly competitive position within it. A word of warning however: unlike the augmented layer, this layer needs to be filled with specific and well-honed added-value elements described and delivered with surgical precision; this is where ultimate competitiveness lies and *this is where marketing and its accompanying creativity can help.* Attending to this layer, the SME can make major strides against larger companies. 'Potential' is the usual description for this 'layer' of the product proposition but this is arguably rarely achieved and *it is incumbent on the SME to be able to appreciate the importance of grouping 'perception' and 'potential' as they both relate to managing and increasing the value and attractiveness of the proposition.*

We look at perceptions and related branding later in the chapter.

So, as we can see from the above, it is not that easy to define even the simplest of propositions, as the market and its perceptions are constantly in a state of flux and can be very subjective indeed.

This means that there is correspondingly a huge amount of room for change, to enhance or refocus on certain key elements of the proposition – and seek an existing 'gap'. By peeling back – or indeed reinforcing – those layers we can determine the complex components of what we provide and start to appreciate what we have, starting with our existing proposition. I have found this exercise most compelling in the past; it opens up a 'huge can of worms' as it allows you and your key people to dissect and forensically examine the whole proposition, perhaps even for the first time.

## Looking at your proposition from the OUTSIDE IN

Take a look again at the illustration of the 'total product' earlier. This is how it appears from inside the SME; adding layers and hopefully, some value. Would it be worthwhile to alternatively take a look at it from the outside in? From the market's perspective?

Your customer or prospect has many issues and problems to contend with, many opportunities to improve and make money that for them remain unrealized. Before moving on to consider how to gauge and improve value, lets take a look from the outside in; the world of the customer and prospect where analyses and research get little further than the extremities of their world, and where suppliers like us *rarely get to address their core needs*:

**FIGURE 7.3**   The total product concept – outside in

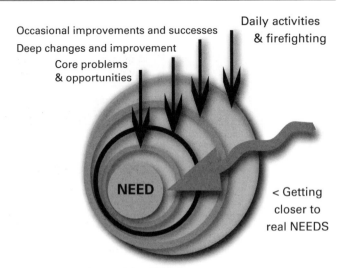

When one examines one's own situation as an SME owner, manager or executive, we know only too well that we rarely get to truly uncover our own deep needs, never mind actually resolving them. We know we spend too much time fire-fighting and performing daily activities to make fundamental improvements to allow us to better resolve problems and realize new opportunities. So people, it is safe to assume that it is precisely the SAME for your CUSTOMER.

 Therein lies the opportunity: to start to see your proposition for the customer and the market, from the outside in. This is worth doing in tandem with the total product approach – and then compare them.

# The value matrix

This value matrix model, adapted from Martinez and Bititci, is used to 'focus business strategy, to select customers and narrow operational focus to value creation in a selected market'. It can also help 'detect some incongruities and suggest some general alternatives'. It is an excellent instrument to help guide the SME to focus on the development of a key benefit and its description:

- product leadership;
- operational excellence;
- customer intimacy.

This model elaborates and improves upon the 'total product concept', to allow assessment and evaluation of tangible and intangible elements; the

**FIGURE 7.4**    Value matrix elements

|  | Tangible Value | Intangible Value |
|---|---|---|
| Product Leadership | Technology Leaders | Brand Leaders |
| Operational Excellence | Relative Price Minimizers | Process Simplifiers |
| Customer Intimacy | Technological Integrators | Social Integrators |

(Adapted from Martinez and Bititci)

next stage from using the value matrix is to develop the proposition further into a true brand and map out the whole marketing mix within a marketing plan. (See Chapter 3 for the marketing mix). This means that the marketer or manager leaves nothing to chance; each and every element of the proposition is mapped out and optimized for the market. The value matrix elements are illustrated in Figures 7.4 to 7.6 then described below.

**FIGURE 7.5**   Value matrix elements (2)

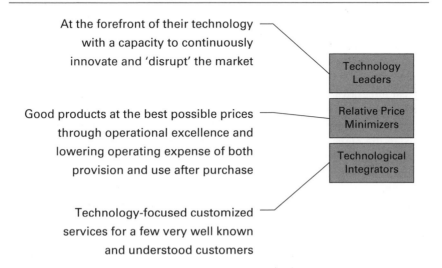

**FIGURE 7.6**   Value matrix elements (3)

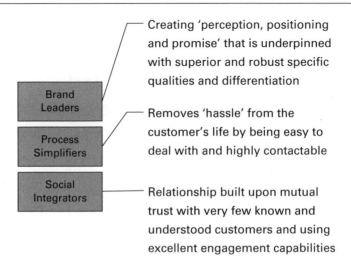

# Notes on using the value matrix

Care should be taken in recognizing that 'relative price minimizers' should relate to operational excellence, not simply purchasing excellence. It is not just about reducing or offering a low or the lowest price, but about increasing gains for the purchaser. This subject is covered elsewhere in this book, but it is essential the reader does not confuse 'operational' financial benefits that are given to the buyer with 'purchasing' benefits; there is often too much emphasis and talk about 'low cost' or 'inexpensive' and, yes, low cost may be a benefit in some cases – but it is a purchasing benefit and may have few or no corresponding operational benefits to add to operational excellence for either the buyer or your own organization.

The categories that are summarized in the value matrix (technology leaders, brand leaders, relative price minimizers, process simplifiers, technological integrators and social integrators) should encourage you to reflect on the current state of your proposition. This is perhaps more useful and true to your own position and help you determine the competitive forces, the 'gap' in the market (if any) and what your aspirations could and should be in terms of where your proposition and organization should actually be placed. These discussions and deliberations would benefit hugely from using *perceptual maps* (see later in this chapter) to help investigate and 'drill down' in to the respective category and help redefine and sharpen your USP.

Similarly, the matrix should be balanced with feedback from the market; remember, true value only resides in the mind and perception of the buyer, not the seller, so you must use these tools with solid evidence from the prospect, customer or consumer.

Of course, different products and propositions can 'reside' in different categories! It is best, though, to keep things simple so that your organization's brand, or its product range brand, does not become confused; you cannot be all things to all buyers, so this matrix should help focus your position in the market, noticeably.

 # Statements and 'stories' supporting the value proposition

The value proposition (the 10 words as described earlier) are best supported by key bulleted points; they must hook the prospect, customer or consumer. These bullet points should be absorbing, not simply some trite 'sales speak', to be able to add credibility and trustworthiness; they can help you later form 'slogans' or 'taglines' to project the key benefits of your proposition.

- *Make them evidential* (ie they must be true and evidenced to a real need or want from the market).
- Use no more than *THREE* key bullet points for a segment.

- *Don't use 'sales fluff'* – every word must resonate and mean something to the market.
- *Say 'so what?'* to all the bullets until they are refined.
- *Test the bullets* to see which resonate the most, and to which target groups of customers.
- *Create some 'supporting stories'* about the proposition: its heritage, source, worth, utility and use, customer input, inspiration etc. Each story will resonate differently with different groups of prospects and customers – so be careful about who you choose to target with the specific story most likely to mean something, and above all be interesting and insightful. These stories MUST NOT simply be about what your company is and what it does. THE CUSTOMER DOES NOT CARE. Keep stories about the company to your discussions with shareholders, internal groups or the bank. Do not share them with your customers unjustifiably.
- *Refine, refine, refine.*

So what is the difference between the so-called value proposition and the product-creation process? Well the proper value proposition contains more than just the development of core product. You will see peppered about in this book references to the whole 'marketing mix' that looks not only at the product, the development processes, the communications and other intangibles and the company's structures, but the value proposition attempts to refine the 'proposition's heritage' specifically and offers the SME the means to firmly do two things: 1) refine what the 'brand' *is* out in the marketplace; and 2) focus the minds of the SME's key people as to what their organization *actually delivers*.

You may have heard the apocryphal tale of the manufacturer of hammers; it sees all customers' problems as needing a hammer to fix them. Every business falls into this trap at some time; witness the bland references in any market to 'solutions' – ie that word invariably means whatever problems you have, 'our hammer will fix it'. This is no good for any SME, in any market; *we have to stand out*. Being seen or promoted as an 'automotive solution provider', 'data solution company', 'logistic solution', etc just means we are behaving like glorified hammer producers and everything 'needs hammering' and 'that is the solution'. Be wary not to use empty words or phrases, or those that could mean just about anything.

## Testing the 'force' of the proposition

Remember, the value proposition with its key benefits is why the customer or consumer should buy from you rather than anyone else. A common misnomer is that the entire proposition is determined wholly logically in some way; but we know that this is particularly hard to do and that even with a sufficiency of good market or marketing research and a good product development and innovation process, *in reality much of it is a discovery process rather than deterministic.*

We should therefore ALWAYS test our proposition; it is arrogance indeed to assume that with all our superb and perhaps even superior skills at coming up with innovative creations that we know will precisely fill some gap or need and that the customer will buy it with open arms. Indeed, not only should we test any product, we need to test any change, improvement or update to any element of the proposition. Sometimes, however, we are terrific at getting some beta-test or pilot product feedback but lamentably less so with the finer nuances and elements of the *whole* proposition – because we see the latter as simply playing with tactics.

Therefore, we do need a means to test our proposition, growing it from meeting an identified and clear need to the development of a wholly defined and competitive package. A key component of our proposition is 'the message' – the *story* that complements the supporting bullet points above – and we need to refine that story into a sentence – and one that will convey, in a specific and relevant manner, the *hook* that will secure the customer and firm up your position in the marketplace.

## Steps to checking your value proposition

1  Intelligence.
   You probably have a lot of information, yet you need to gather some more. You have an idea of what the proposition should be, but temper that with evidence from previous work that included campaigns, customer feedback, metrics that you have used in the past (use this opportunity to check that they are appropriate measurements too), competitive dynamics of the market (and where you are currently and where you could be). And of course, use the tools contained within this book to test that what you think may be important is actually real competitive intelligence.

2  Create draft propositions.
   This sounds like a lot of work, but it needn't be; if you have performed the earlier evidential checks to show that what you have is profound evidence and intelligence based on market needs and wants, then you are in a very good position to construct alternative propositions and tabulate them.

3  'Measure the force' – to work out how your proposition may fare in the market; measure against, where you can, word of mouth from the market and get customer and prospect input into your proposition options. You can test with the salespeople, agents or channel partners and those who have direct customer contact to help refine those

outline propositions. Test those optional outline propositions using the following criteria:

- *How desirable are the propositions?* Do they actually appeal to the market, rather than to you?
- *Are they exclusive?* Can the market buy this proposition anywhere else apart from you? (The value of your draft proposition goes right down if they can get the same elsewhere.)
- *It is entirely credible?* Would your people be happy delivering the proposition as described?
- *Can the draft proposition meet the tests* outlined in previous pages that allow for a great story to be told and establish some outstanding key bulleted-benefits to be honed, as primary competitive advantages?
- *Would the prospective customer find the proposition truly unrefusable?*

**4** Test.
Using inexpensive channels and ways, test your refined proposition. This is an opportunity to not only test and optimize the proposition, but to identify and refine the ideal prospect. Even though you may have thoroughly researched your market and evidenced your new or modified creation, you will need to refine somewhat your description of precisely who is more likely to buy.

**5** Target.
Remember, that good refinement might mean that you feel that you are ignoring or giving up some potential market segment of group of customers; but although that feels counter to your very soul, this is key to maximizing impact on revenue. There is no point, after all, in having a great competitive advantage if you are looking at the wrong market or customer and ignoring the one that you – and perhaps only you – can best serve.

 *Giving up some possible business to focus on targeting probable business, means defining and refining a strong perception of excellence for your proposition in the market and intuitively makes sense.*

**6** Use metrics that matter, to measure – remember these 'Ms'.
Not all metrics and measurements matter; more on that later. Make sure that your metrics work for you, not the other way around. This is as important at the test stage as well as when the proposition is out in the market.

**7** The proposition should only take several seconds to describe.
It is no use having long-winded propositions; you must be able to convey the proposition succinctly and with surgical precision.

**FIGURE 7.7** Testing the force of the proposition

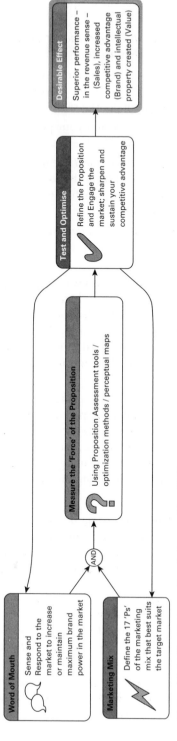

The 'desirable effect' – the outcome you wish – of your test regime should be to improve the proposition in such a way as to exhibit:

- superior performance (increased sales potential);
- increased competitive advantage (strong brand);
- creation of real intellectual property (value).

A unique, quick and helpful tool to use before and during testing of your proposition is the Competitive SME *'proposition accelerator' tool*, explained later in this book and available on the Competitive SME website resource.

## Using 'focus groups'

I tend to pause and sigh when I hear the phrase 'focus group'; I am certain that you do too. It seems to be the marketers' favoured phrase and the solution to just about everything! I would caution about using focus groups and placing too much faith in their ability to do anything worthwhile.

I suppose the best you could say about them is that it gets some of your prospects or customers together and you can meet them; at worst, it can be a costly activity and may result in 'findings' that are truly skewed and simply give you the results that you wish to see. They are too expensive and risky if all you are ending up with is a distorted validation of your previous perceptions or misconceptions or if you end up simply performing this as 'going through the motions' of research or customer-related activity that was expected of you.

What I would favour instead, is using technology to its best effect; using it to grasp, secure and involve your market and have it converse with you in a way that *the customers* find attractive and enjoyable and that you find valuable and endurable.

You can use simple feedback and conferencing systems that have *immediacy and a better context for feedback*; through-the-web conferencing and virtual-discussion groups can be hosted simply and easily, and much can be achieved without the cost or risk that bedevils a traditional focus group.

Quickly constituted online meetings mean quick results; quick feedback can be achieved on immediate problems and opportunities and as they offer some degree of immediacy, can prevent or stop you making costly decisions at an earlier stage and keep your campaigning or proposition development path on track for success.

'Branding is not simply an issue for big business. It is critical as a means to competitiveness for the SME and not as difficult or complex as one would think.'

In any case, testing the 'force' of your proposition is an ongoing activity, not to be done solely as a reaction to some trauma or specific commercial problem; it should be done continuously, feeding from the WOM process into the development of a competitive marketing mix. Those elements over time can then be optimized for best results.

## SME\ 'Branding' and 'imagineering'

OK, let us grasp this 'thorny subject' now, once and for all; *branding is NOT JUST AN ISSUE OR ACTIVITY FOR 'BIG BUSINESS'* or something for large, international consumer-goods companies. This is an increasingly important matter for all SMEs just the same, and indeed is arguably even more important for the SME that is seeking to be more competitive.

Why is branding more important for the SME than the large corporation? Because the large company can throw money at promotions, has many outlets and channels and plays the numbers game – if it throws sufficient resources at promotion, then someone will surely buy. That is not good enough for the SME who needs, more than ever, to know that every penny spent on acquiring new customers and keeping them does just that. Your brand is increasingly important as it embodies all your value proposition, marketing mix and key advantages and delivery elements that your customer values; the components that 'craft trust' and a preference to do business with you.

Branding is thought of as being very challenging – a blend of art and luck with a bit of creativity thrown in – but is it that difficult for an SME to utilize some rudimentary branding nuances to help improve competitiveness and revenue? No, it is not hard at all.

*As far as the SME is concerned, branding has four main aspects:*

- It is important in helping to adequately DIFFERENTIATE your proposition.
- It can be counted as a substantive part of your proposition and 'worth' as a company.
- It creates a 'tangible' perception of value that otherwise may not be so well conveyed or visible.
- It aids in 'force and projection' of your proposition into the marketplace and its positioning within it.

I have also used the word '*imagineering*' to convey the message that it is just as important an element of logical, constructive and precise creation as is the process and thought behind the engineering of a product.

## A short 'brand parable'

This is a simple yet good example of the subtleties of branding. A commercial airline pilot has a bad landing and some exceptional turbulence during one flight. He has already had to endure a couple of recent flights that have proven less than enjoyable and indeed the weather and flying conditions, for him at least, seem to have never let up for quite some time. Unlucky of course, as weather does change, but this run of bad luck does happen. One of his air stewards has been on a couple of those flights, with the same pilot. This steward is relatively new and unseasoned; he is not used to so much anxiety about flying even though he knew that flying in the cabin crew would be like this.

If this new steward flies with the pilot a few times, and witnesses what he thinks is more than his fair share of turbulent flights, will it be long before he blames the pilot for his bad experience of working on an aircraft?... And perhaps more interestingly, how long would it be before this steward passes on his belief about the poor capabilities of this individual pilot to others and the pilot gains a reputation and starts to be referred to as 'Captain Bumpy'? How is that for an example of a 'brand' without foundation, formed only from perceptions and word of mouth?

 *'Brands are not created or made, but cast.'*

This 'parable' demonstrates that perceptions are vitally important, and hard to contemplate or precisely manage. However, a major step is knowing that perceptions do exist and can be influenced positively and convincingly. Take a look at how important branding is to the SME in Table 7.1 and how it relates to business effectiveness for SMEs, compared with larger companies, and the differing opportunities that it creates:

**TABLE 7.1**    Branding and the SME

| Branding element | Large Company | SME |
|---|---|---|
| 'Values' | 'Global' and playing to their institutional investors and the 'city' | 'Personal' in that they mean something to the owner / management and to certain long-term or engaged customers |
| Trust and Confidence | Often cynically 'manufactured' and reinforced by constant campaigns | Earned the hard way, yet can be neglected by the SME |
| Benefits | **Projected** to the market and tempting | **Experienced** by the market and affirming |
| Application | Broad, diverse range of products and businesses | Narrow, limited to single offerings or the company |
| Service & Administration | Impersonal and cold | Personal and warmer |
| Technical support | 'Evolved', systematic, yet passive and cynical | 'Unevolved', ad-hoc but necessary |
| Relevancy | Can always find a market somewhere | Has to be specifically relevant to niches |
| Value perception | Determined in large part by competitors' pricing | Determined by what the SME thinks it is |
| Positioning | Large budgets spent on influencing the buyer and building market pervasiveness | Trust, 'closeness' and reliability are key to a strong position as is being 'specialist' |
| Consistency | Can afford to change tactics and branding elements indefinitely | Must focus on key attributes and agility of response |
| Product/Service Portfolio relationship and structures | Can adopt mini-brands for each product in the portfolio; produces and offers multiple lines | Must focus on specific, narrow-band product lines and more intimate service add-ons |

**TABLE 7.1**  *continued*

| Branding element | Large Company | SME |
|---|---|---|
| **Spread** | Branding appears everywhere, from PR and promotional activities to simple everyday elements such as invoices, to build and maintain the brand | Appears very sporadically and is not tightly corralled; everyone is not working in concert to maintain or grow the brand and it is vulnerable |
| **Understanding** | Have qualified marketers who know about brand and usually have 'big brand' B2C or B2B experience | Have little in terms of branding speciality, but can build on its position and communications very effectively |
| **Longevity** | Brands are supported with long term development and strategic growth plans that are accordingly well resourced | SMEs tend to work in shorter cycles, so there is a major opportunity for them to build longer term relationships and a more enduring brand |
| **Measurement** | Evolved systems including psychological and behavioural assessments and aspects clearly managed | SMEs can, and indeed should, only measure what really matters; opportunity exists to have a highly focused brand |
| **Warranty** | Straightforward; usually favours the *company* rather than the market | Complicated; should favour the *market* |
| **Complexity** | Very complex activities and strategies; **simple things often overlooked** | Very simple strategies; **simple things make all the difference** |
| **Communication (of the brand)** | Multi-channel and everywhere | Sporadic and only on promotional media |

© Copyright David James Hood: Competitive SME

The 'source' of your brand story can be quite different and potent as an SME. What is significant is that SMEs have less resources and experience in 'creating' brands from scratch; SMEs need to embrace a simple process to identify and nurture their brand and uncover the brand elements and attributes that *matter* and those that can be developed. Investments in 'brand' value can result in more value to the business than you may think; *we all have a tendency to consider investment in the technical and tangible development of products and services as 'more real' than any investment in brand and perception management* – but the figures would tell you a different story. Investment in the 'brand' is just as important to the SME as investment in 'technology' or tangible innovations. We have to make sure that we redress this imbalance, but likewise, we need to ensure that we are identifying and developing the RIGHT brand elements and attributes or we may end up doing the opposite of what we intended! *We need structured and nurtured IMAGINEERING!*

> SME⟩ *'Brands and branding are arguably more important for the SME than for the large corporation.'*

Let us now take an uncomplicated look at how branding can help you, the SME, ensure that your own positioning – the place you have in the market linked to the perception of the customer and prospect – can be better cultivated and entrenched.

We need real marketing, real brands, brought down to earth and 'imagineered' through relentless, evidential needs-determination.

 ## What can branding do for me?

- It is more than solely looking at your 'vision' and 'image' or 'defining what business you are in'; it is about positioning in the mind of the market, prospect, customer and consumer.

- It can give your company and the product or service a 'character' that results in competitive positioning in the market that is both clear and valuable.

- *It ties EVERYTHING up together* – all the strands of 'what you do', what you provide, why anyone would wish to do business with you, 'what's in it for them' – and gives you the *basis and opportunity to grow and maintain a real presence and force in the market rather than 'just being present'*.

- It makes your pricing policy and the value projected for the product, a lot more believable and supports higher pricing.
- It helps develop a trusted and higher profile in the mind of your channel partners downstream, over other potential suppliers that compete with you.
- It can help you secure a 'preferred partner' status over other suppliers.
- It helps the consumer develop a preference for your product.
- It reinforces your value to any prospect, customer or consumer and consequently aids the process of maximizing good word of mouth.
- It helps create a barrier to entry for a competitor and builds a distinctive difference between their offer and yours.
- *Every time you have a meaningful and deliberate conversation with your customer or consumer you are adding to your 'brand' and increasing your value to the market and the value of your organization.*
- *A differentiator or USP can make the basis of a good brand; likewise, a good brand can help make the basis of a good differentiator or USP.*

 *'Brands and branding are arguably more important for the SME than for the large corporation.'*

# SME branding: perceptions, positioning and segmentation

One cannot start to develop or enact any branding strategy without first considering the related areas of positioning and segmentation. Whilst considering your strategy, and how you would wish to address your market (see Chapter 5 and Ansoff's matrix in particular), we can examine what your markets are and could be, through determining the different perceptions and values placed upon our products and propositions. Different types of prospects, customers or consumers will view our offerings very differently and the elements of the marketing mix would have to change to better suit those specific niches or market segments.

Of course, the old way was pretty straightforward: look to see where your most obvious groupings of customers or consumers were to be found and 'tailor the presentation to them'. Now though, things have markedly changed; your customer may not be that obvious, may be contactable or not, may be 'found' in many different places and by so many means. And of course, they are developing an increasing awareness of their own needs and can now seek and find what they want rather than having to rely on the producer to inform them of what is available. This means that an entirely new approach to segmentation is needed. Indeed, though, many aspects of both segmentation and positioning remain and it is not too difficult to grasp any changes and make them work for us.

# Getting branding right

- Stick to a small number of brands.

- Read up about 'brand equity' (this is important, as although it does sound like another piece of marketing-speak, your market is buying more than just a product or service; reading up on this subject will pay back huge dividends, and this form of 'equity' is valuable to you).

- *Remember that informing the market, or making some prospects or customers aware of your proposition, is not the same as ensuring that they have the correct and strong image as to what it is, what benefits it conveys, or why and how it is distinctive from other propositions.* It is easy to fall foul of thinking that the market should know 'your brand' as you have promoted to it. It may simply know of the existence of your core product, service or elements of your proposition, but may not be wholly aware about what it means, or should mean, to them directly.

- Realize that your 'push' and 'pull' branding activities and campaigns are two distinctly different issues; your immediate customer buys for very different reasons than your ultimate end-use consumer. Your brand should represent and recognize those differences.

- Branding activities, like your marketing strategy and planning, must lie at the highest level of your business – so branding needs to be understood and championed by someone at board or owner level.

- Co-branding – that is, branding performed in conjunction with other partners, suppliers or customers themselves – is an underused source of branding and possibly offers financial and material help in providing this important function.

- Ensure that your brand's 'representations' (logos, stories, colour schemes, messages etc) are to be found and are consistent wherever there is a 'touch-point' with your customer and supply chain (all paperwork and communications, vans or delivery vehicles, uniforms etc)... and of course, the actual PRODUCT!

- In addition to a 'brand champion' at senior board level, make a specific person responsible for day-to-day management of the brand and incorporate this role and process into your quality assessment and management systems.

- Check if your product brand is better or more important than your company name; check and make decisions carefully. Your reputation and differentiation depends on a careful choice.

- Other 'problems' and issues within the company may be preventing brand development and the creation of a good brand; identify these issues and areas first – your brand has to be 'lived and breathed' by everyone in the organization, equally. It is more than a 'diktat' or suggestion to all employees and as a manager or owner, you have to 'live it' too – and lead by example. If you wish your brand to espouse some clear characteristics and say something about your organization, it has to say the same about you and your people. *The brand must link you, your people, your proposition and the market all together.*

- Be consistent – in how you manage your brand and what messages are conveyed over time.

# Important evolution of modern segmentation

**FIGURE 7.8**  Evolution of segmentation

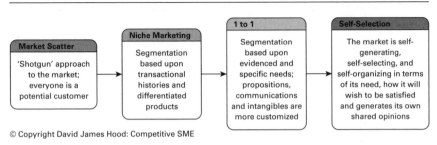

© Copyright David James Hood: Competitive SME

Segmentation is a word that percolates marketing and business; it is certainly a primary and important marketing activity and process that can yield major benefits to the organization and its market. It helps reduce waste, improves branding, propels propositions into the market, develops distinctive USPs and improves return on investment for marketing, sales and arguably all organizational activities. It is a valuable tool in the SME marketing toolbox.

That said, it is easier said than done. At least it is easy to do some initial and superficial segmentation based on the simplest 'qualities' or profiling characteristics of certain parts of the market. Nevertheless, this is necessary but insufficient.

We must realize that large-scale, wholly homogenous market groups as we understood them *do not exist anymore*. Even among the largest collection of prospects, customers or consumers that do show some common features, they actually have as individuals many underlying and quite different needs, wants and reasons for selecting and buying. Not only that, but when you consider many SMEs act within a B2B (business-to-business) environment, the SME should consider that even if some of its customers down the supply chain buy similar products, they don't necessarily have the same buying reasoning, the same decision-making or buying processes, the same customers, or indeed receive the same operational and financial benefits from your proposition.

Likewise, just because someone or some organization has bought previously, that does not mean that your previous marketing assumptions have been validated; it is dangerous indeed to see a segment just as an aggregate of buyers with the main common thread that they have 'bought the same product or service in the past'. Customers and consumers are more than mere transactions and markets are more than aggregates of those historical transactions. Markets, and indeed needs, move too fast nowadays to tie down a whole 'market' and keep it stagnant and within some arbitrary category determined by us.

*'Looking at your market predominantly through the perspective of resources, rather than need, results in flawed segmentation.'*

*Hence, the advent of '1-to-1' or '1-2-1' marketing*: the recognition that everyone, and every company, buys for very different reasons, has very different benefits from the 'Ps', has different perceptions, requires different variations to the propositions over and above the standard or core product (or even the enhanced or augmented one); and in especial, the B2B customer needs very much a 1-2-1 approach. Building and maintaining 1-2-1 relationships is becoming increasingly recognized as the best means to stave off competition and help bolster longer-term relationships with your individual customers. It is obvious to people in business, and SMEs in particular, that to foster 1-2-1 relationships is better than treating the 'whole' market as one and the same – but we often fail to do this operationally and we do not apply that common sense when we come to conducting marketing and sales activities.

The development of 'CRM' in tandem with 1-2-1 marketing and segmentation is important, and to combine both in a meaningful way can help develop a USP and a powerful position in the market, thereby leaving less to chance and building the perception of your proposition. So far, 1-2-1 has perhaps not realized the aspirations for it; it has resulted in a more accurate targeting of messages, but achieved less in terms of actually listening to the market and responding better to it. *We may have sharpened the message, but we haven't realized that communication is two way and 1-2-1 is much more than simply adding some fields to our CRM system and putting information into it thereafter.*

CRM should have given us the ultimate 'customer personalization' mechanism where the customers or consumers decide upon what proposition they wish, how they would wish it constructed, how and where they would like it to be 'delivered' and what kind of contact they would wish (or not) with our organization and supply chain. A filled-in field in a database is neither a true understanding of customer need nor the basis for a *human* 'relationship' between our organization and its customers and consumers.

Now we come to the latest evolution in segmentation: one that reflects the advent of 'intra-market' communications, self-organization of buyers, prospects and others into what could be said to be 'true niche' segments. These 'communities' can range from simple ad-hoc interactions online with interested parties exchanging information on possible goods and services, right up to complex co-buying consortia that can establish both very specific needs criteria and huge aggregated buying power. The 'consumer', or at this time 'domestic', social networks are growing and being complemented by evermore evolved business-to-business peer networks and this is only the start.

We cannot afford to ignore the fact that business has to be done in those social and professional networks, as the crossover from consumer social networking impacts B2B in an increasingly profound way. Professional buyers are no less keen to short-circuit research and buying-decision processes, looking for ideas, results and buying validation from their peers, tightening requests and opportunities for tenders and proposals from their respective supply chains down to the chosen few; the landscape of the way we do business is fundamentally changing and we need to grasp that change.

##  Perception is EVERYTHING to your customer and the market

Never a truer phrase was said. The cynical advertising world knows this – that is why they bombard the unsuspecting customer or consumer with wasteful messages; likewise that is why some politicians and their 'spin doctors' work with the premise that if you tell a lie often enough, it will stick and become a truth.

I am mentioning this here to simply underline the fact, but just as telling the truth is a valuable policy for the SME; there is virtue and profit to be made by using this facet of human nature in the right way. It can also help us make better decisions and ensure that we make and deliver what people want, as well as what they may actually need.

When customers or consumers buy a product or service, from you or elsewhere, they buy it for a number of reasons. *You may probably not know what most of those reasons are.* Indeed, in B2B sectors, you would think that all purchase decisions and actions tend to be extremely logical, having been made by 'professional buyers' with all their formal processes and exacting requirements.

*'Perhaps, in the modern marketplace, it is more advantageous to view the market in terms of engagement and being engaging rather than demographics and traditional segmentation.'*

What we tend to forget is that they are *people* first. 'People buy from people' and in this world of ever-increasing competition and with barely a minuscule discernible difference between alternative suppliers as far as the customer or consumer is concerned, *perception is key to attracting and securing new customers and keeping existing customers you would wish to hold on to.*

*'There is almost always a competitor down the road that can offer pretty much the same product or service; business brands have only their brand reputation to rely on.'* (Scot McKee)

Remember: what *you think* is a major difference, what actions you carry out and what proposition you provide, is probably not what *your market thinks* at all.

They have their own perception of you (personally!), your company and your proposition. And indeed, their own perception of their world and its challenges and opportunities.

If you buy in to the reality that word of mouth is the most powerful tool in creating, maintaining and growing business and 'your brand' in the market, then perceptual matters are of the utmost importance as part of your effort to engage with the prospect, customer or consumer.

Looking back at Chapter 4, and 'leveraging what you have', there are only a few key benefits that your existing proposition or new sufficiently updated proposition will have that will be of any importance and higher value to your current or newly targeted market. It can help to map out those benefits in very simple terms as comparative perceptions, to see where the gaps are or could be between your proposition and your competitors' or current proposition and customer need. The gaps and differences can then be readily seen, expanded, improved and – most importantly – tested. These gaps or differences can then be sufficiently buttressed and sharpened to develop and sustain major competitive advantages.

## Perceptual maps

There are a number of differing types and permutations of perceptual maps that an SME can use; what is worth considering here is how we can quickly and readily look at the macro elements of the market as well as the micro.

An example of a 'macro map' is the degree to which a service is given over and above the provision of a core product (see comments regarding the 'Total Product concept' earlier in this chapter) and a 'micro map' is where two specific major and evidenced benefits or competitive advantages are compared. These can be used to map out existing propositions and planned or possible options for an 'idyllic new product or service', or simply to update and modify existing propositions.

These maps can lead to development prioritization and testing in your market and save a lot of time and money. Also shown is not only just the 'gap' as mentioned above, but the relative 'distance' between your possible offer or current proposition and where the competitor propositions are or could be located. These maps are key indicators and useful tools for achieving precise brand testing and management.

Figure 7.9 is a traditional and *simple* perceptual map. Figure 7.10 is a product/service mix: an example of a '*complex*' perceptual map. This 'macro map' offers an assessment and insight into the dynamic and nature of the product/service ratio with levels of commoditization/customization for some different sectors.

**FIGURE 7.9**    Perceptual mapping

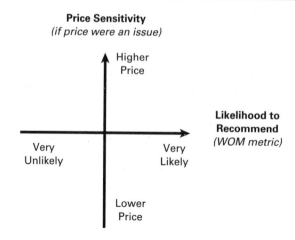

**Price Sensitivity**
*(if price were an issue)*

Higher
Price

**Likelihood to
Recommend**
*(WOM metric)*

Very
Unlikely

Very
Likely

Lower
Price

**FIGURE 7.10**    A complex perceptual map

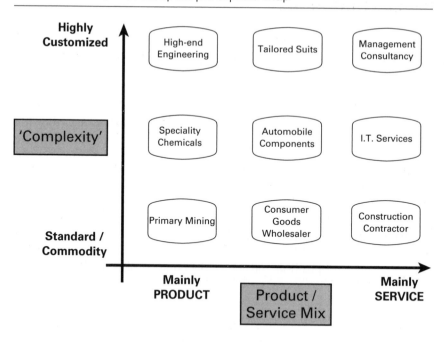

**Highly
Customized**

High-end
Engineering

Tailored Suits

Management
Consultancy

**'Complexity'**

Speciality
Chemicals

Automobile
Components

I.T. Services

**Standard /
Commodity**

Primary Mining

Consumer
Goods
Wholesaler

Construction
Contractor

**Mainly
PRODUCT**

Product /
Service Mix

**Mainly
SERVICE**

Caveat: it is sometimes very difficult to place 'you' within this type of map, but it is useful to check against competition and customer/consumer perceptions and expectations (eg 'software' can either be in a standard/product or customized and service-heavy 'space').

The example in Figure 7.10 is, of course, somewhat subjective; it is very difficult to 'group' a sector or type of product or service, especially in today's highly competitive and complex world. Indeed, this map and how it would be organized and respective sectors placed may be somewhat different for every customer or consumer. That does not however diminish the power or relevance of perceptual maps as a great tool for positioning, finding gaps and ensuring that you have the best proposition in the eyes of the market. They are a very good aid to helping the SME focus on material advantages, and indeed questioning 'what market you are in'. *What this means however, is that it is singularly important that you use the market's definition of any two or more axes and their perceptions of where certain sectors, markets or competitive propositions are situated on those axes; and that the descriptions and axes are not of your own devising and based on your assumptions.*

Resulting potential areas for development and differentiation can be transcribed to a RADAR map, such at that used with the Competitive SME proposition accelerator tool (See Competitive SME website for details).

*'Customers and consumers are grasping, harnessing and celebrating their ability to use word of mouth to their advantage, way ahead of commercial organizations.'*

Perceptual maps are very useful tools, both before and after the development of a 'USP': before, to check and look at ideas for USPs (to see if indeed a niche may exist) and afterwards to gauge and map just how genuinely 'unique' and strong the proposition is. *There may be no 'ideal' but a range of maps can be used powerfully and sharpened using word-of-mouth indicators and dimensions.*

Of course, the above is merely an example of the many different variables you may wish to test. It is a good way to not only help position your proposition, but also to check the relationship (if any) between two variables in the market and the interaction between them.

A cautionary note: the areas within perceptual maps are rarely exclusive and easily or precisely defined, as many differing propositions or descriptions can be interpreted differently or readily placed on a map. For instance, on the second of the two perceptual maps, the position of the two propositions 'management consultancies' and 'IT Services' could arguably be swapped on the map, depending on the type of client served, the clients' requirements and how they are being met.

An oft-quoted interaction between two variables is the issue of price and market share. It is habitually (and sometimes wrongly) said that if you drop your price, then your share of the market increases. This is arguably wrong in many cases, and we are not discussing that issue here; but these two variables are often mapped and relationships are often developed to show some degree of 'elasticity' between two variables, which in turn helps you to react to those relationships and maximize your position through managing the perception of your proposition within the market.

When your proposition or one of its variables is mapped out, a degree of differentiation can be established; this can be used for continuous and worthwhile market sensing and reappraisal activities (and with relatively low costs), which are simple to set up and maintain. You can use these maps also to check your own perceptions against the harsh reality of the market, before and after some action (eg after a survey, conducting an advertising or mailing campaign, changing your proposition slightly, using some promotional methods, examining trends etc). You could also use these maps to position and check ongoing changes in competitor activity and behaviour, in a meaningful and useful way. You can check trends in perceptions as they change, branding and competitive manoeuvring and its consequences. *Additionally these perceptual maps can actually be fun!*

Many examples of perceptual maps you may come across are variations of 'quality v price' – but beware of using bland and ill-defined terms or metrics such as 'quality'. In the case of this type of map, one would have to have a definitive descriptor for the 'quality' axis in terms of a *specific* benefit or proposition and consider that different pricing strategies may be used as opposed to a single one, as different pricing strategies are usually applied to different markets.

 *You can create a simple brand management 'system' based on developing your 'killer USP', calibrated using perceptual mapping and word of mouth management, and thus create and manage a great story or narrative that the market finds suitably attractive and engaging. And ensure that all of the above is developed and refined in a suitably potent marketing mix.*

The resulting marketing intelligence created and nurtured will be as important in terms of an intellectual property asset in your organization, as in its tangible 'smarts', 'how we do things around here', good efficiency processes (lean etc) and other 'codifiable' production advantages such as designs, patents and process or operational systems.

# A simple brand management cycle template

A simple brand template is given below (this can be used in conjunction with the section in Chapter 4 'I just don't have anything to say'). The branding exercise translates all of your work from your research, through value and proposition development, to help you project your proposition into the market and ensure that the whole proposition is where you would like it to be positioned in the minds of your prospects, customers and consumers.

*This can help you to PROPEL and accelerate your proposition in the market and fend off the competition.*

**FIGURE 7.11** Brand management cycle

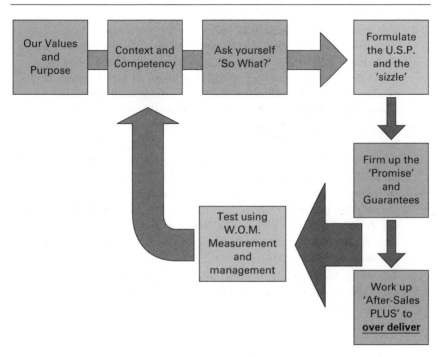

© Copyright David James Hood: Competitive SME

**1** Our values and purpose:
   What we strive to do and how we do things differently to help our markets achieve their objectives, and make a real difference.

**2** Context and competency:
   What we are positively known for in our market; what we would wish to aspire to be and how we are developing as an organization to reach those goals and capabilities.

**3** Ask yourself 'so what?':
   Refine what you are saying about your organization and your proposition. The market must have some great reasons for buying from you; this helps with your narrative and 'story' development.

4 Formulate the USP and the 'sizzle':
   Identify the hook and the key competitive elements. What are the main attractive components of your proposition? (See the earlier section about statements and stories supporting the proposition). You will have to do some creative branding activities such as 'developing the look' – logos, colour palettes etc – but keep all those creative works simple and honest and ensure that all the respective elements chime together and work with your marketing mix. (See Chapter 3 for the marketing mix.)

5 Firm up the 'promise' and guarantees:
   You may be able to articulate the above to your prospect or customer. They may not believe you. You need all the evidence at your disposal to prove your USP; indeed, you need to guarantee that it will be delivered and they will gain a major benefit from it. This means planning for 'reluctance to buy' or some well-rehearsed responses to ensure that your USP is believable and accepted.

6 Work up 'after-sales PLUS' to over-deliver:
   Tell the customer that they are, or will be, on your 'After-Sales PLUS' programme; this ensures customer satisfaction, keeps them involved for feedback, ongoing improvements and new developments, and most importantly, gets them onto your customer panel. This is essential for guaranteeing to your market that you mean what you say, and that you can and will deliver; it also gives you the WOM channel you need to measure your 'brand' and support and develop it now and in the future.

7 Test Using WOM measurements and management:
   Tests all your 'have dones' and feeds back to highlight any necessary future changes to your proposition and brand (see Chapter 12).

## Social networking and 'the new reverse customer convergence and segmentation'

No book on modern marketing and competitive advantage would be complete without a section on 'social networking'. Those various (predominantly online) groupings of prospects and customers (although they may not see themselves that way!) are people and organizations with common interests, all looking to be satisfied, informed and improved, and generally seeking what they need and want. This definition is an attractive opportunity to SMEs that would wish to provide to those communities. Arguably, again, SMEs are better placed to meaningfully engage with and deal with 'social' communities' needs and wants; the nimble SME can delve with very low cost into any kind of community and engage with them with little risk or expense, other than time.

The largest fundamental issue and change is that 'social' – let's call it that for the purposes of this book – has brought about a real, actual *'customer active paradigm shift'. It is putting the customer and consumer in control.* What was shown earlier in the book is that the 'power' has moved from the manufacturer down through and to the distribution chain, and correspondingly from product focus to sales focus, with power ultimately residing with those who could shout the loudest and most directly at the customer or at the early evolution of the 'marketing focus'. Social has meant that the era of the customer has finally and indelibly arrived and is changing business.

 HOWEVER, we have to be truly marketing-led before we can grasp social networking and make it work for us.

The customers and consumers now actively communicate with each other; THEY are grasping new and assertive ways to interact, harnessing and celebrating word-of-mouth AHEAD of commercial organizations! Although this activity could be said to be predominantly B2C (business-to-consumer) at present, B2B (business-to-business) is maturing rapidly. Remember, even the 'professional' business buyer is still an individual human being and will inhabit online groupings and perform research on the internet with certain key groups of influencers and fellow 'users' and buyers. The WOM world now has its own 'untameable, irascible irrationality' – and this is something that *BIG COMPANIES JUST DO NOT UNDERSTAND.*

Big companies cannot control it, so they simply try to shout louder to their customer social communities or networks; and at best, they saturate those groups and communities with messages. Big companies with big budgets are plainly falling into the same old trap, yet again. SMEs can really win here, as many are by their nature and size, niche players... *niche is essential in the new socially connected world of WOM!*

Social should be seen by the SME as a fundamental and unprecedented opportunity to listen, respond and be involved with the whole supply chain. Even with the end user. It may be an opportunity to 'rehumanize the brand' where you and your partners desire stronger brand acceptance and resonance within end-user markets; but 'rehumanizing' can happen only if we do not succumb to overcomplicating matters and communications with new technology, or use technology as a surrogate for good old-fashioned one-to-one conversations and engagement.

SME\ *Let us go back then, to 'brain-to-brain' communications where both our humanity and our favoured form of interaction reside.*

# Managing the 'social' media: engagement

According to B2B marketing specialist Scot McKee (of Birddog), there are three main elements to social media marketing; this gives us a convenient model to manage our activities and presence within the 'social' arena. In addition to recreating Scot's 'Social Trinity Model' (Figure 7.12), I have used his examples of the media and platforms components and recommend they be used in conjunction with the other marketing tools in this book.

**FIGURE 7.12**    The 'Social Trinity' model (McKee)

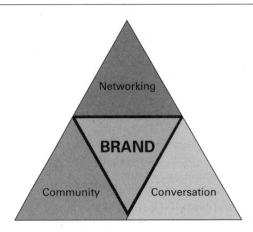

This simple model shows and reminds us of the valuable components that we need to use 'social' as a *means of engagement*. It is of no use whatsoever to think of social as just another way to 'shout at the market' – we have to manage it in conjunction with our new convergence on WOM as the main metric to guide revenue and reinforce our competitive position in the market. Table 7.2 outlines what the SME can do to address the onward progress and challenges of social media.

**TABLE 7.2**    Strategic objectives and focus for 'social'

| Social Component | Objective | Focus |
|---|---|---|
| Networking (eg LinkedIn) | To be able to find and be found in your markets | Establishing authority and influence in the market |
| Community (eg Facebook) | Collections of individuals and organizations with common interests | Engagement platform to position your offer and add value to the community |
| Conversation (eg Twitter) | To be able to hold meaningful two-way communications | To solicit feedback, action and activate 'viral' Word of Mouth |

To use 'social media' effectively, it needs to be a formal part of your marketing plan (see Chapter 8 for marketing planning) and firmly managed on a consistent and constant basis. These 'social components' are of course not mutually exclusive, in that their objectives and focus overlap and will change with time and use. What is important though, is to consistently assess what impact they have on your business and the market and how communication is conducted within it. If you don't understand it, or do not wish to have to worry about having to manage it, there are people aplenty to help, from specialist outsourced resources to even some student looking for a project!

The important point is that you do have to become *engaged* in social. Like it or loath it, it is here to stay and extremely powerful, pertinent and personal.

 Consistency and frequency are more important characteristics for social than they have been for traditional media; people that 'inhabit' networks and communities and have 'conversations' all have an expectation that, whatever they experience, whenever and whoever they connect and converse with in their social networks and communities, *anyone who would connect with them and offer propositions, would do so in a way that doesn't just interact with their network or community or speak with them only when they have something to sell to them.*

Social media is so new and could be seen to be a formidable challenge; I do not wish to suggest it is or can be anything other than complex. But what we need to remember that although it allows us to do many things that were not possible before the advent of the internet and digital marketing channels, the basic good marketing principles still apply. It is a real opportunity to 'rehumanize' your organization and its contact with the market. It forces us to look at the person rather than 'consumer', or at the B2B organization as a group of people rather than just a 'customer'. I do hope that 'social' offers and encourages us, over time, to be less fixated on the competition and more on those whose custom we would wish to secure. Our 'competitiveness' depends more on relevancy and our relative 'engagingness' rather than attempting to shout louder than our competitors, thanks to conversations within communities and networks. Social also allows you a genuine and fantastic opportunity to *LISTEN*.

You can now get first hand, individual and collective experiences and a flavour of people's needs and wants. You can observe as well as listen, and see how trends are affecting the market and may affect your brand and proposition. It also helps you align your 'story' as described earlier, to the market. It gives you an unprecedented opportunity to identify and engage with the large number of influencers any market may have; you could look to become a major influencer, and your social media strategy and activity within the marketing plan should fully reflect this. It is worthwhile having a section of your plan dedicated to engagement with influencers within the communities and networks in addition to consumers or customers. Of course, influencers are now often the customers and consumers themselves!

The important point to consider is that we no longer have to guess who is influencing our market – we can see and hear them in action!

*'The excellent companies are better listeners'.*

(Tom Peters)

**FIGURE 7.13**   Chapter 7 summary action table

| ☑ | CHAPTER 7 Summary Action Table |
|---|---|
| ☐ | Map out notes against 'Porters 5 Forces' specifically looking at who and how, uses 'power' or influence to shape your environment |
| ☐ | Consider what research is required to facilitate the creation of a good Marketing Plan or your immediate campaign, improvement or new product/service |
| ☐ | Decide who is going to conduct research, how and when |
| ☐ | Take advice and before you run your research, test what you intend to do with marketing advisors, trusted customers and agents, and some other people you have identified as 'influencers' in your market |
| ☐ | Identify a good source of feedback; customers have shown an interest or complained for example; set up your research or customer 'Panel' over and above your research target respondents |
| ☐ | Workshop: strip down your product/service that is an issue for you right now; strip it down to the core through the layers. Likewise, look at the 'outside in' layering – involve a few carefully chosen customers if you can |
| ☐ | Position where you think you are and where you would like to be in the Value Matrix and use alongside Perceptual Mapping to triangulate possible areas for competitive advantage and a 'good story' |
| ☐ | Write your story around the Proposition, its layers of product/service, the needs fulfilled and why it is better than the competition; refine it as fully as possible |
| ☐ | Check the current and preferred 'brand' with the SME Branding Elements table; any gaps or improvements? |
| ☐ | Test your Proposition with a small part of the market; use the brand checklist: 'Getting Branding Right' |
| ☐ | Sharpen the 'brand' and your proposed USP with further Perceptual Maps around some differentiating characteristics that the test market has realized and do the same for your key competitors |
| ☐ | Formulate a simple, but effective, Brand Management process as suggested and diary in to manage and use it again later, using all of the above steps, to refresh all |
| ☐ | Check how the new digital media and social 'channels and platforms' will affect all these steps and activities listed above and factor in to your Brand Management process (especially 'storytelling') |

© Copyright David James Hood: Competitive SME

**FIGURE 7.14**    Summary of the essentials from this chapter

| What to **CHANGE** | What to change **TO** | **HOW** to change |
|---|---|---|
| • How we react to change in the market by using sporadic campaigns<br>• The disproportionate time we spend on examining our competition<br>• The perception of our product and the attributes we place on it<br>• We lead with features when promoting our offer<br>• We use little 'branding' tools and philosophies<br>• Little understanding of the power of perceptions<br>• Passive and indifferent attitude to 'social'<br>• Deliver to what is expected | • WOM is our means of sensing & responding<br>• We spend more time looking at our customers' needs<br>• The perception of our proposition in the market is well understood and valid<br>• We lead with evidenced benefits when pricing our offer<br>• An understanding of 'our brand' and how it can help shape our presence and impact in our market which neatly ties up 'all that we do and provide'<br>• We use social to affect and inform our WOM and viral marketing<br>• A realization that perceptions are as, if not more, important and powerful as what we think is our reality | • Use a WOM process to gather knowledge, capture new needs, better survey and sense, and manage an enhanced profile & position in the marketplace<br>• Refine the proposition using the marketing mix<br>• We have a process to build & measure the 'force' of our proposition in the market<br>• Study the significant aspects of brand building and (Simple) brand management for SMEs; be consistent in how we manage, develop and sustain the brand, internally and externally<br>• Get some help with social marketing!<br>• Understand how our customers and consumers perceives our offers and 'value' and analyze often |

© Copyright David James Hood: Competitive SME

*"We lived on farms, then we lived in cities, and now we're going to live on the internet!"* **THE SOCIAL NETWORK (MOVIE, 2010)**

# What do we really need to do?
## 08
## Planning to win

> *Managers are spending too much time managing the present and not enough creating the future.* **GARY HAMEL AND CK PRAHALAD**

The above statement is perhaps true. But our day-to-day world of managing an SME is all too focused on 'the now' – the fire-fighting and reactions that face us daily – dealing with the clear, immediate and real problems that confront us constantly.

If we find ourselves overcome with the daily routine of fire-fighting and 'getting things out of the door' then we have little time for future (or market) gazing; but as we explored in the earlier chapter on 'stress', we do need to separate out what we should and shouldn't do to reduce personal stress – and this will give us time and capacity to grab hold of the company's helm and direct it accordingly. Again, that is easier said than done. What I have done in this and the preceding chapter is address marketing planning and research, to help you know where you are and where you could be in your market, and to implement your marketing plan. I have also offered a summary table later to promptly deal with some major specific issues you may have to address immediately.

## Investment in sales and marketing capabilities

'Don't confuse the art of the possible with the art of the profitable.'

(David Tansley)

One of the major challenges for an SME is its sales and marketing capacity. It usually has few salespeople, and many SMEs do not have any marketing people, formal training or resources at all. This book of course does not cover marketing skills or training in depth, but it would be useful for the SME to explore what marketing skills it *needs* to develop, based on the gaps identified during the course of applying the tools contained in this book, and using the results of the Competitive SME and online resources (if indeed, you have completed any activities on the futureSME website).

For completeness, should you wish to explore improving practical marketing skills further, information is available that was created by the Marketing and Sales Standards Setting Body in the UK and documents on specific marketing skills can be downloaded from the UK Standards site: **http://www.ukstandards.co.uk.** We plan to support and build upon those standards within the Global Marketing Network – follow the book's twitter (@CompetitiveSME) to be kept up to date.

# Marketing plan and planning: it is not just writing a document for the shelf in your office

Marketing planning is a critical step in increasing the likelihood of commercial success for your organization. A good marketing plan certainly does not guarantee success, but as the old and wise saying goes: those who fail to plan, plan to fail. That is never truer than when it is applied to working-up commercial propositions and tackling markets.

It does, of course, always seem like a bit of a chore to compile and enact a full marketing plan. In practice, they are usually little more than a series or sequence of marketing campaigns, loosely strung together to look like some kind of strategic hand is guiding the process. The SME pretty much always falls foul of insufficient planning in addressing and aligning its proposition with the market; again, like 'strategy' it is seen as something that large corporations have the capacity to perform, but SMEs do not have the time or resources to carry out. This is fundamentally wrong but, interestingly, is a real source of advantage for the SME. I have personally experienced medium-to-large organizations that have no strategic or marketing plans; they flounder and follow the market rather than setting the pace of it. They were, and remain followers, picking up the scraps from the market and they have an endless list of problems, in large part of their own making.

A marketing plan is a major step in improving your competitiveness – and sustaining it, as it is a working document: something that not only sets out your firm intentions, your purpose, and robustly improves your fullest and best proposition ensuring clear rewards for those who buy it, but also makes sure that you nourish and sustain your developing 'brand' and hard-won position in the marketplace over time. It is essentially the best means to ensure protection for your strategic investments and maintain your organization's resilience.

# SME When writing your marketing plan

- Realize that your most obvious, 'easiest' or traditional market is not always the best one for you. (The same goes for individual customers you may have or desire.)
- A well-researched and formulated strategy must comes first, before tactics.
- The process and plan should include all people and processes that are 'touch-points' with the market, whether they are located within the company, in the customer or prospect market further down the supply chain, or 'influence' the market in any major way. There must be input from operations and all those who 'make' the proposition what it is.
- Your plan should be about alignment; what you can do to remove, resolve or reduce some of the real problems in the market or help secure some major opportunity for your prospect and customer.
- A 'gap' in the market is not just a space or void to fill; there may be a void for some very good reasons!
- A true gap is where an unaddressed and evidenced need is clearly defined and articulated and results in improvement for your customer and consumer at the exclusion of other 'voids'.
- Involve everyone: the customers and all people that serve them. This should be a priority to all in the organization: no customers, no salaries and no shareholder or owner dividends!
- Avoid a preoccupation with the 'short term'; it is important to manage income generation in the near future of course, but you are trying to build and sustain a long-term distinctive and resilient position in the market with a suitable and continuous income stream. So fight the temptation to try every tactic imaginable and 'tweak' the proposition.
- Spend sufficient time 'getting it right'; otherwise you may spend a lot of time mopping up the mess from getting it wrong.
- Be very careful when considering 'market or industry reports' or generic trends and information from 'soothsayers' in your markets; most forecasts tend to be very wrong (and useless) and the best forecast you can get is the evidential one secured from your customer or consumer.

- Decide what tools you intend to use to gauge and research the market opportunity; consistently use the same measurements afterwards to gauge the change and activities undertaken and subsequent efficacy of your strategy and campaigns.

- Likewise, determine what overall measurements are important, how you are going to ensure that they are consistent, when they should be undertaken and by whom.

Place in your plan all of the results of your assessment and analysis using the tools in this book and from those found on the Competitive SME website.

It is important when you are actively using your plan, updating it or indeed revising it later, to know why you came to certain key decisions and to carry out further work that may reflect or contrast with your previous findings. You can use the tools again to recalibrate your plan and activities as part of a new, ongoing and exciting process of ongoing improvement.

 # Components of a great marketing plan

## *Executive summary*

This section must not only summarize the work to be done or work that has already been undertaken to sense, survey or explore your market or the campaigns and actions you intend to undertake; this should be the substantive and key part of any business plan and is best constructed and considered to be a *working* document.

'Working', in that it is not just a 'report' or some repository for your intentions or options, but that it will be referred to daily and updated and amended accordingly. You need to use it to manage return on investment and to aid improvement to ROI constantly. If either your business or marketing plans sit on shelves or are only consulted and updated occasionally or annually, then expect to be months or even years behind your competition.

The executive summary is a one-page section that outlines what the plan does; it should summarize your intent: what markets you are actively engaging with, what the killer proposition is, your 'elevator test' proposition description and how you plan to improve and sustain your competitive edge in your markets. The plan itself should contain all of the elements in the previous chapters; a brief summary action table and outline of key results can be placed in here too.

It should start with where you are; a summary of your SWOT analysis, followed up by where you wish to be. The 'how' part can come later within the document itself, other than offering a brief indication of what the killer competitive advantage is that you need to secure or develop in order to realize the objectives laid out in the plan.

Numbers are great – and expected – here. However, be careful about 'finger-in-air' targets and other financials and figures. All figures should be evidenced by the findings of your previous research work and engagement with the market.

This summary should also include:

- what the plan is for (activities, strategy, what it will do for the organization's health and wealth now and in the near future);
- who it is aimed at (stakeholders and whoever is going to be involved in providing input and, later, seeing it through);
- time factors and references to ongoing strategies and other overlapping and complementary projects and activities;
- the top-line financials (maintaining or improving revenue and profit);
- where it fits in and addresses components of your futureSME™ strategy map (see the futureSME™ site for details of how to create and use one).

## Return on investment (ROI) statement

This is a general description of what the financial objectives are and an overview of how they will be achieved: how they will be paid for, how much they cost and what ROI is anticipated. This would include a statement on why some course of action is to be commended, and correspondingly why it is the best course of action rather than others. (All this is thoroughly worthwhile as the marketer or manager will be asked questions on these subjects constantly!)

Remember, an ROI statement cannot be only about your campaigning, brand, product or market development responses; it must be backed up by facts that make the reader – your colleague or board and of course, yourself – know that what you are undertaking is going to get the best returns.

This again helps as you may be up against other competing or conflicting initiatives or ideas that require financing and you need to prove that the money is better spent on this project than any others.

## Objectives

- What are the objectives that will lead to the goal of the ROI target(s)?
- These are the top-level 'end game' results that will lead to money; they have to be more than the usual simple 'get more responses back from our campaign' kind of objective. 'More responses' may not be sufficient to be turned into cash; everyone needs to know how your activities will turn into cash.

- These figures and the substance behind them should reflect a distinct refocus on effectiveness of marketing activity in addition to efficiencies; if you are looking to ring-fence budgets from limited funds, then it is important to demonstrate not only that any investment will be wisely spent, but that it will give a similar or greater result than what has been spent previously on marketing activities.

- Be VERY clear about what you need to measure and check to make sure you are measuring the correct metrics, again and again, using clear and correct measurements as your objectives.

## Clarifying objectives

Your objectives need to be further drilled down to identify and clarify the intermediate objectives, actions and activities that need to be undertaken to achieve them. The example given above of 'achieving more responses' is actually more of an intermediate objective and needs sufficient clarification if such is used.

This is where, like this book, you can apply the sensible and simple construct of 'what to change', 'what to change to' and 'how to change'. In effect, this provides you with your strategy, your intermediate objectives and your marketing plan.

You can use some of the tools contained in this book (such as the SWOT analysis) to define what is standing in the way of achieving your objectives, what changes need to be made and what shortfalls have to be addressed; carefully check any assumptions that require to be fully challenged and even overturned before progress can be made to implement the plan. Feed in your SWOT findings to see what objectives are needed to deal with SWOT issues. Two examples of using this approach are given in Table 8.1; this method clearly gives one a *strategy* (What to change), intermediate *objectives* (What to change to) and a *marketing plan* (How to change).

## Marketing research

Check the paragraphs earlier in this chapter and headline what you wish to achieve from your research to fortify your marketing plan. (Re)determine the 'value proposition' in terms of what the customer would distinguish as true value and the *gap* in terms of your existing knowledge and what you need to know to make confident decisions to support your efforts to achieve the objectives. Your marketing research should *always* support your key objectives; otherwise the plan will go awry and lose its focus and chances for success. Be aware that research should not simply reinforce any existing assumptions about your market, product, position, delivery or customers and prospects. It should be used to TEST those beliefs and not just validate received wisdom or some unsupported hunches.

**TABLE 8.1**　Strategic objectives and marketing planning

| What to Change (Strategy) | What to Change to (Intermediate Objectives) | How to Change (Marketing Plan) |
|---|---|---|
| Poor position for our brand against the main competitors; the Prospect or Customer doesn't always know the true extent and value of our offerings | Our preferred Prospects and Customers have us on their 'approved list' and know the difference between our offer and others and value it accordingly | • Define what the customer's perceptions are now<br>• Study the underpinning reasons for that perception<br>• Check and define the need of the customer as it relates to their expectations<br>• Work backward and review the development of 'added value' from the Customer to our 'Production' process<br>• Outline a change plan that will improve and clarify the offer and which will genuinely refine and amplify our USP<br>• Review our process for getting on the Customers approved list and educate the Customers' Buyers with our new well positioned offering<br>• Define what changes will be made to the marketing mix |
| Our pricing policy is preventing us getting more business; we are seen as 'too expensive' | The Customer genuinely values our offer, and has no problem paying a price that makes us money and they see as a terrific investment | • Our entire product and proposition has to be broken down into its constituent parts and reviewed<br>• Each part is to be tested against Customer input and Feedback<br>• Each part is mapped out to see 'what's in it for the Customer' for each feature and benefit<br>• 'Which means that'... and 'so what?'<br>• Testing our Proposition to ensure that we focus on the major ROI for the Customer and add only necessary features or benefits that evidentially add major value<br>• Check that we are being recognized for any 'freebies' that we may be giving away that are valued yet not reflected clearly in our proposition |

Remember: the purpose of your marketing research should be to see further, more clearly and definitively than other organizations and influencers in your market; it is to enhance decision-making, particularly relating to proposition improvement and the necessary investment in resources that accompany it. Indeed, good marketing or market research exists to LOWER STRESS on you and the organization and to increase confidence in your organization, for both you and your customer.

'Forecasts' from your research should not simply be made top-down 'from the board', based on figures from the previous financial year (or other period) with a little more revenue added to account for the fact that everyone wants to make more money than the previous period. Your well-defined and accomplished research should give you all the real forecasts you need. A forecast on sales and income is best seen as a guideline, one that changes throughout the course of the period and, as you move forward, becomes more and more agile and can change with the market – rather than after it has moved on. You can adjust your forecasts in real time. Current, real-time forecasts that are based on insight and clear, immediate and developing needs are more useful than forecasts that set targets in advance simply based on adding something to the last period's figures. Oh, and stay well away from 'the current market is X billion; we will target a 0.5 per cent share of that' kind of meaningless goal. What you want to do is make the most income you can regardless of size of market, what share you have within it and how big you are. As an SME, it is critical to think niche not 'small', and beware of turning megalomaniacal with outrageous targets of capturing a huge slice of a very competitive market!

 *'A gap isn't just a space in the market; it has to be a fundamental and clearly defined unsolved challenge or unrealised opportunity' for you and the market.'*

## Current product status and innovation

Of course, as an ambitious and reinvigorated SME, you will have a number of product propositions out there in the market already, some at early stages of development, some getting somewhat tired and perhaps even to be withdrawn when replacements can be found. So any improvement to your current competitive situation has to take full cognizance of those current offerings, and an assessment of their evolution using the traditional marketing tool the 'product life cycle' (PLC) would be thoroughly worthwhile

**TABLE 8.2**   Marketing research

| Research aspect | Consideration |
| --- | --- |
| Goal | • **Clearly defined**, for the research component of the plan; does it aim to maintain and increase income or is it exploratory? It must help us make money and be aligned with the Plan's Objectives |
| What Market? | • **Define what the market (or collective 'target respondent group') actually is**; if it is new it may be poorly defined; but we need to know if we are looking for the right market in the right place at the outset |
| 'Marketing' or 'Market' Research? | • **Marketing Research**: checking our proposition and what changes we should make to it to enhance our current market status and presence, its importance to the market and income opportunity and to help optimize the proposition<br>• **Market Research**: exploring possible new market(s) to create, develop or move into it |
| Types of Research Required | • **Primary**: *original research* – who we need to speak with and determine core challenges and opportunities (our prospects and customers)<br>• **Secondary**: what published, or *publicly available* information exists and who has it, which we will need to harvest in order to check the other effects on our Plan (see Porters 5 Forces in the previous Chapter) |
| Important Contacts | • **Who and where are the people** we will secure to help gain an insight and from whom we will harvest our intelligence? |
| W.O.M. | • **How this will all feed into your WOM / CRM system** *(more on that later)* |

within your plan. This would allow you to explore, evaluate and prepare the company to enact your plan whilst being entirely practical and addressing your current product 'portfolio'.

Although there is an explanation of the PLC below, it has been updated somewhat to include the modern marketing and competitive policies and ideas put forward in this book.

The product life cycle – an illustration of the cyclical nature of products in the market and markets themselves – shows that there are usually distinct phases, each with different dynamics relating to customers or consumers, challenges and opportunities and marketing strategies and tactics to increase, maintain and elongate the income stream from a product or product line. This is where your tools can be employed to gauge changes in perceptions and to the strategic context for the SME, along the course of your product's 'lifetime'.

These phases along the curve could be sales, market size relating to your product or the whole market, or indeed the number of sales or income from the market. PLCs are said to follow similar patterns. What is most important is that you use the PLC to help manage your relative presence in the market, specifically to check where your product, product line or proposition is in relation to the curve and possible strategic or tactical manoeuvring along it. As Figure 8.1 suggests, it is of course financially worthwhile to both heighten and elongate the curve in your favour!

The various phases are self-explanatory; they can vary according to the overlap between phases, different descriptions of the phases and the type of company, industry or market sectors in which they are employed, and how they are measured.

Essentially, the PLC phases act as a tool to remind us of a number of key competitive marketing aspects and dynamics:

- It is best to proactively identify, maintain and manage the phases of the PLC as best you can (otherwise the competition and customer will do it for you).
- Along the lifetime of the product, it can be checked where it is relative to other products in terms of ongoing robustness and 'perishability', calibrating and recalibrating the path along the curve.
- It reminds us that the product alone is not the entire proposition, and that the wider proposition needs nurturing to keep the product at its most competitive.
- It helps us map out our competitors' products and their changing strategies and tactics to improve their cycle or their place in the market (elongate the growth, mature, or decline phases and of course, if possible, 'elevate the curve' in terms of sales revenue all along it).
- We can plot our progress along the curve and do so for all our products and use it as a simple planning tool to check our current and future strategies and tactics to maximize income.
- It stops us prolonging the life of a very dead product and proposition!

**FIGURE 8.1**  Maximizing the product life cycle (PLC)

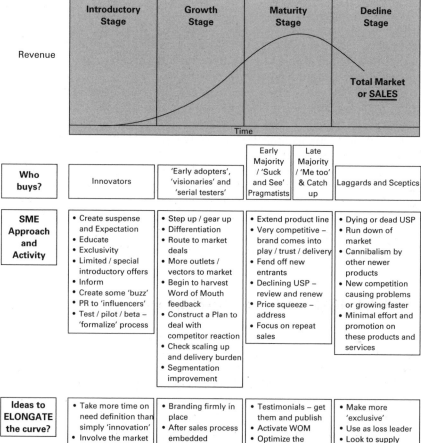

| | Introductory Stage | Growth Stage | Maturity Stage | Decline Stage |
|---|---|---|---|---|
| **Who buys?** | Innovators | 'Early adopters', 'visionaries' and 'serial testers' | Early Majority / 'Suck and See' Pragmatists \| Late Majority / 'Me too' & Catch up | Laggards and Sceptics |
| **SME Approach and Activity** | • Create suspense and Expectation<br>• Educate<br>• Exclusivity<br>• Limited / special introductory offers<br>• Inform<br>• Create some 'buzz'<br>• PR to 'influencers'<br>• Test / pilot / beta – 'formalize' process | • Step up / gear up<br>• Differentiation<br>• Route to market deals<br>• More outlets / vectors to market<br>• Begin to harvest Word of Mouth feedback<br>• Construct a Plan to deal with competitor reaction<br>• Check scaling up and delivery burden<br>• Segmentation improvement | • Extend product line<br>• Very competitive – brand comes into play / trust / delivery<br>• Fend off new entrants<br>• Declining USP – review and renew<br>• Price squeeze – address<br>• Focus on repeat sales | • Dying or dead USP<br>• Run down of market<br>• Cannibalism by other newer products<br>• New competition causing problems or growing faster<br>• Minimal effort and promotion on these products and services |
| **Ideas to ELONGATE the curve?** | • Take more time on need definition than simply 'innovation'<br>• Involve the market from the outset<br>• **Change to emphasis and measurement of income, not transactions** | • Branding firmly in place<br>• After sales process embedded<br>• Encourage customers and prospects to talk with each other<br>• **Focus resources on determining different 'customer currencies' regarding your proposition** | • Testimonials – get them and publish<br>• Activate WOM<br>• Optimize the Proposition's 'Marketing Mix'<br>• Long term incentives<br>• Promise and guarantees<br>• Low cost or free upgrades and modifications as they become available<br>• Product extensions<br>• 1-2-1 marketing<br>• **Use WOM to increase 'likelihood to recommend'** | • Make more 'exclusive'<br>• Use as loss leader<br>• Look to supply 'cheaper' or less discerning markets<br>• Find those who consider switching too costly to undertake<br>• Decrease the rate at which the product may be considered 'obsolete'<br>• **Review and update the constraints for your customer and the market** |

Note: all these ideas for actions to elongate the curve or react to changing market and sales dynamics are not exclusive to each section; they are merely offered as an indication of the type of issues likely to be more important at certain times, than at other stages.

The four stages are sometimes augmented with a fifth that precedes the others – the pre-market stage or research and developmental phase. This is where money of course goes out of the organization, where the product development happens and marketing research is undertaken. It is not that helpful to include this in the PLC other than to remind ourselves that we need to ensure that the area under the x-axis of the curve is more than complemented and negated by the area above the graph to keep the finance director or accountant happy with some ROI!

That precursor stage is where the existing customers and prospects can be 'interrogated' for their needs; 'suspects' can be clearly ruled in or out as 'prospects'; blue-sky thinking and innovative brain power is brought to bear; bottlenecks are identified internally in terms of our ability to deliver to the market, or externally in terms of constraints that our customers may have. Of course, if we already have a good WOM/CRM process in place, this part of the PLC curve should be exciting and productive rather than experienced as risk, cost, stress and running on nothing but hope. Clearly, this is where the risk can be reduced markedly, and helped of course by creating and implementing a sound marketing plan.

... Therefore, the 'old' PLC is still a very useful tool!

# Positioning and perceptual maps

As explained elsewhere in this book, perceptual maps and their variants are powerful and key tools to determine where we are and where we could or wish to be. Your plan should include current and later – future – maps and your 'how to' sections should spell out precisely how the current perceptions and positioning can change and define the 'gap' that exists and would be exploited. Remember, a gap is not just a space or void; it has to be a fundamental unsolved challenge or unrealized opportunity for you and your customer. Your plan requires an assessment and prognosis regarding the findings of your research and how this directly relates and aligns with the developing 'position' statement – ie where you, and better still your customer, think your proposition is in the market place relative to other offerings. Your positioning using the results of these maps and other tools should be clear and unequivocal; you need to know where you are and where you wish to be, and exactly how this measures up against your competition.

# The core challenge and conflict for your customer

This section deals with what you have defined, or need to redefine, as what could be the customer's, prospect's, consumer's or market's most fundamental need – the one that will result in you making the most impact on them and which makes them and you the greatest return.

This is not always easy to do; there are some tools and other options within the futureSME™ initiative and associated website resources, but one cannot skirt round the fact that this needs some hard work. The downside? Well, it takes some guts to sit down with customers and talk frankly and candidly about how the supply side (including your organization) may have failed or overlooked some key elements and issues that exist for them and which are inevitably leading to less effectiveness for the chain.

You can come across as very unusual, and indeed may provoke some customers to think that you are simply undertaking yet another cynical 'consultative selling' exercise. The upside? You are not consulting; you are gaining an insight WITH the customer rather than seeking how to manipulate them. Once they see the effect of their discussions (through proper and clear feedback of your results to them), how you are sharing their objectives and joint rewards, they will see the benefit of a true partnership based on a new currency. (See Chapter 9 about 'changing currency'.)

 Remember, it is very easy to fall into the trap of focusing on established purchasing benefits rather than operational benefits to the customer! Find some meaningful operational benefits in 'the gaps'.

## Developing your proposition and propelling it into the market

- List the changes necessary within the organization to match the new market opportunity.

- Identify the 'hot spots' – the stories and other aspects of the brand that the market would find not only of interest, but crucial to their own intelligence and benefit – linked directly to their core challenges and opportunities! (And do not have them guessing how your story is linked. Draw a storyboard and make it very clear!)

- Determine what channels you will use to effectively 'market' your proposition; identify where these channels are, what target customers may be found there, how to get the best ROI from each channel and what suitable messages and other modifications to the marketing mix and proposition would be required for different audiences (remember, no customer or consumer is really the 'same').

- Fill in the table for the marketing mix for each channel or sector you wish to address. (Again, not all elements of the mix would need to change though, so this need not be too onerous; list the key USPs that may be a benefit and are critical to your customers in each segment.)

- Prioritize your 'touch-points'; each and every change to the proposition and application of your ongoing marketing efforts will change the profile of what you need to resource and support at these points, as the plan is enacted. Also remember, the change may result in a change in 'touch-points'. Many plans fail as they are heavy on promotional activity, but light on supporting and harvesting the goodwill and interest subsequently generated (a great example is how poor most organizations are at following up prospects acquired at an exhibition event).

- Time periods are essential; in planning, we have to know all of the above, but we have to also know WHEN. Take a look at the sales side too (see Chapter 10) and improve how the sales funnel can function and be weaved into your marketing plan. After all, it is no use activating a marketing plan without involving and engaging with the sales function and people, and ensuring that your activities chime with theirs.

# Results

This section of your marketing plan begins with an aspiration and, as the campaigns and changes are progressed, checks are made against targets, the status of the project reported and any changes identified that could be made to improve the ongoing plan. This section would also outline who is to receive ongoing updates relating to the efficacy on the plan, any changes to it or any controls necessary to be added to improve its ongoing implementation. Remember again, to involve the sales process and people in your chain in this, so that marketing results in empowering and optimizing sales activities, so that salespeople and agents are not simply playing catch up with your activities – or having to second-guess them!

# Action plan and schedule

The plan of course is not just an embodiment of your intentions; it has to show the course of your activities, when they will be enacted and what sequence they will follow.

Remember to factor in a 'between-sales' plan of engagement with your customer or consumer; don't just rely on contacting them as part of your cyclical sales plan or when you want to ask them for money! A between-sales plan can be even more effective than a discrete sales or marketing campaign. The action part of your plan, and accompanying schedule should contain the elements outlined below.

## *What we need to change*

### Outline of your overall STRATEGY

- our touch-points with the market; mapped interfaces from market-facing people (including those what are not seen as being 'in commercial touch' with the customer on a regular basis such as the receptionist at the front of the organization and anyone involved in product development, support, delivery etc);
- understanding of our market: where it is and where it is going;
- perceptual maps;
- marketing audit;
- PLC;
- our existing marketing mix... etc;
- changing our whole perspective to one of need determination and resolution.

## *What we need to change to*

### Outline of your INTERMEDIATE OBJECTIVES to realize the plan

- resources; including any training or 'upskilling' needed with specific components of marketing qualification or education for specific improvements, roles and individual 'touch-points' with the market;
- Clear, evidenced and prioritized intermediate objectives; all objectives should leads to greater or sustained financial health for the company and delivery to its listed stakeholders. These should link directly to the development or nourishment of the competitive advantage.

## *How we change and realize our opportunity*

### Our marketing plan (remembering to include any early stage PLC development work and results)

- what tactics we will employ;
- what strategic and tactical tests will be carried out on the market (to experiment, refine and optimize our proposition) and how we will measure ongoing results and make refinements;
- who we will engage with, how and when;
- how we develop our 'irrefusable offer' and how that is/was specifically aligned with evidence of a core need(s).

**FIGURE 8.2**  Chapter 8 summary action table

| ✓ | **CHAPTER 8 Summary Action Table** |
|---|---|
| ☐ | Construct a Marketing Plan |
| ☐ | See what marketing skills you can easily identify, develop and employ from the UK Marketing & Sales Standards |
| ☐ | Check your existing research – what is public knowledge and your previous work, involving others; use the simple template provided |
| ☐ | Carefully write your Plan, starting with *what to change*, *what to change to* and *how to change* |
| ☐ | See what research gaps exist and undertake further research |
| ☐ | Revise your Plan and Test it |
| ☐ | Revise it again and Optimize it |
| ☐ | Keep returning back to the Plan at least once a month – it is a ***working*** plan after all |
| © Copyright David James Hood: Competitive SME | |

**FIGURE 8.3** Summary of the essentials from this chapter

competitiveSME™

| What to **CHANGE** | What to change **TO** | **HOW** to change |
|---|---|---|
| • Lack of planning for marketing strategy and activities<br>• Little or no consistent or constant marketing research<br>• We react to the market to try and defend and maintain the proposition's duration in the market | • We use a good, comprehensive Marketing Plan and Planning process to effectively engage with our market<br>• We understand how to use marketing research, as the means to improve and maintain return on investment for our marketing and sales activities<br>• We have a managed, proactive process to launch and sustain our propositions in the market and reduce obsolescence | • Create the Marketing Plan<br>• Use it as a **WORKING** document<br>• Update it with results, lessons learned and 'include all the stakeholders in its creation'<br>• Realize that the Plan is a 'how to change'. Your strategy is 'What to change' and your objectives are 'what to change to' to make ROI crystal clear and simplify your Plan<br>• Make clear and definitive marketing research a foundation and ongoing basis for a good Marketing Plan<br>• Use constant and consistent methodology (but again keep it simple)<br>• Act upon your research, to help calibrate where you are now and where you could or would wish to be<br>• Elongate and heighten the PLC<br>• Use the Marketing Mix and Value Proposition tools to maintain a truly competitive offer |

© Copyright David James Hood: Competitive SME

*'Shun the incremental and go for the leap of faith'* JACK WELSH

# Grasping the opportunity 1 (MARKETING): 'Changing the currency'

"When all think alike, then no one is thinking. **WALTER LIPPMAN**

## What is the primary pain for your customer?

Remember that your supply chain – those further down the line that buy from you and supply to the end customer – is not there simply to 'push product to the customer'. You have to give your immediate customers a major advantage in turn, if you hope to secure your position with them. In this book I have argued that there is little point in simply tinkering with the product or proposition; we have to address some fundamental need for the market and to do that we have to drill down to establish 'what the pain is' and how we can markedly change what we find. Only then can we make a leap forward ahead of the competition.

Business leader Dr Eli Goldratt put it succinctly, using price changes as a simple example of tweaking with your proposition. He maintains that if you:

- Change price, your competitor reaction is one day.
- Change a 'rooted policy' for your customer, the competitors' reaction time is up to two years.
- If you change several rooted policies, your competitors' reaction time could be up to 10 years.

Changes in an organization's proposition usually last only a few days, or perhaps weeks, in terms of its ability to stand out and have a distinctive USP that is comprehensively competitive and robust. Looking at Dr Goldratt's assertion above, what lead on your competitors would you rather have?

If marketing, as described in this book, can lead to changing some rooted policy in your environment, would that be worth investing in? If that 'rooted policy' better reflected improving operational benefits and capabilities for your immediate customer rather than purchasing capabilities, *how much more could you now charge?*

# Moving to a 'change in currency'

Can we really fundamentally change the way we do things, so that we come out on the side of the customer and consumer? This is no academic and highbrow discussion; *this is an almost unique opportunity that is rarely grasped and yet is where the best USP and revenue generating possibilities lie.* Simple questions start to stimulate us to think about 'changing our currency':

- Can we move closer to the customer or consumer, in terms of delivering what they regard as a successful proposition?
- For example, can we alter the way we deliver trials or test products so that we can check their efficacy at achieving success, based on the customers' or consumers' valuation and their ROI measurements?
- Can we change from determining how 'successful' we are, based on or around our conduct and activities in attempting to hit sales targets, to something more fruitful?
- Is our process of enquiry > to proposal > to demonstration > to test > to changes in specification or features > to approval > to sale, good enough?
- Do we have bottlenecks in our sales process? Do we see a large drop-off in numbers in our pipeline as we go through the process? (You can use radar charts to compare where your percentages change through the funnel.)
- Look: 1) at ratios in the funnel; 2) the 'yield' (efficiency in moving from one point in the process to another); and 3) lead times (can we maintain the first two, and reduce the third?)
- Can we change the sales process to a revenue machine? (See the next chapter.)
- Can we also change to an elegant and powerful new way to identify the customers' currency, in a similar way to the example given later in this chapter?

*'Change a "rooted policy" for your customer, the competitors' reaction time is up to two years'.*

(Dr Eli Goldratt)

For SMEs, change – especially in manufacturing – should start with a major and fundamental shift away from our compulsion to concentrate on *margins*. A focus on margins leads to an unhealthy approach, dysfunctional behaviour and antagonism within the supply chain; *it fosters a view that your supply chain partners (your own suppliers and your customers) are combatants*, all looking for a larger slice of a finite (and ever decreasing) margin. This addiction to margin has to cease if the SME is to break its shackles and really change to the 'currency of the customer'. They have to change forever this 'deeply rooted policy'. This, as the above statements show, would mean quite a change to the way you have done things in the past; but it can lead in turn to a change in several 'rooted policies' and result in a real and lasting competitive advantage.

*A major advantage lies in changing your proposition and strategic direction towards not only the 'need' of the customer, but wholeheartedly towards aligning your SME with the customers' currency. Destroying the 'addiction to margin' is a MAJOR and indelible leap forward to improve your competitiveness.*

In addition, changing to the customers' currency can prevent us making tweaks to strategic and tactical activities (that are usually made in desperation) and performing actions that are not making any money.

## 'Moving from margin myopia'

*'My customers, and their customers in turn, are not buying as often as I would like and in a way that leaves me with sufficient margin; indeed my margin is ever decreasing.'*

If we fixate about margins, *we lose our purpose*; we are not in business to create 'margins' nor are those margins any more than a function of cost-plus and cost-accountancy. We want and need to be paid for our efforts to create value. That is our purpose.

So, if it isn't about margins, what exactly is the 'customers' currency'? How can we successfully and meaningfully divert our attentions and stresses associated with our perpetual quest to gain some share of a 'finite' margin, to something more productive?

The essence of the matter is related to what has already been said in this book about how our perceptions of what we provide are wholly out of synch with what our customers' perceptions are of us; the related policy or hurdle misalignment is that we consider we get paid based on how much we sell to the customer. Your customers in turn, get paid on how much they sell. *But, we both actually sell different things.* Your product and entire proposition is not what the ultimate customer receives nor the same as what the partner provides down (or indeed up) the supply chain.

**FIGURE 9.1**    Necessary conditions to change to a new 'currency'

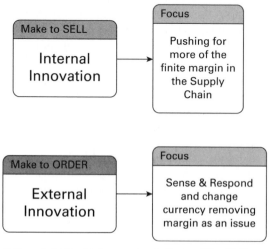

© Copyright David James Hood: Competitive SME

Margin does not reflect 'value' and is nothing more than an incrementally added portion of the ultimate selling price – so how can we progress from a fixation on margin? Part of that change involves a move to reflect 'innovation' as it pertains to our creativity out there in the market rather than to our own 'internal' creativity. *This can help us correspondingly shift gear in a way that could be described as moving towards 'making to sell' and away from 'making to order'.*

- When we focus on margins, we are focusing on the wrong subject; we would be better placed examining value down the supply chain – at the very least between us and our immediate customer.

- *A fundamental change from purchasing benefits to operational benefits for the customer.*

- Assess all of your customers' 'content requirements' in the timeline – ie what they need to know and when – along their buying 'journey'.

- See 'innovation' as more than making you different; it has to gain for the customer some major operational benefits.

- Change from taking orders based on features and price to win–win value development (see next few pages for a terrific example!).

The use and value of the product and experience of the wider proposition is different along the chain; it's not just the price and margin that differ. Ultimately, we only see the last and final user – the consumer – as someone who pays an amount that equates to the sum of margins all the way back upstream along the supply chain. There are, however, real and elegant competitive opportunities in seeing things as the customer does and changing our proposition and currency accordingly. The example below is a fantastic exemplar of 'changing to the customers' currency', and is a real story.

Whilst I do question the usefulness of case studies (in that no organization really has the same problem, clearly defined and shown to be the precisely the same as another, so why suggest the same solution), I will however eschew my reticence and use the story as a good example that powerfully illustrates real change from a margin and cost-plus approach to one of 'value' and related pricing that grasps and exploits the 'currency of the customer'. And it created a fundamentally differentiated edge that the competition couldn't and wouldn't match.

 *Consider the following real-life account; could you emulate this company and 'remove a standard industry annoyance', removing some real pains? If you can do that with your own company, in your own market, with your own customer, using his or her own currency, it will be more productive than copying any conventional case study!*

## Changing the currency: an illustration

A major laboratory service specialized in the analysis of samples from a variety of sources, from food and water supply through to sewage outfall and industrial waste, but badly needed to revitalize its position in the market and pull in more sales.

It had a clear and present challenge: although its service was highly rated by the customer base, it appeared to be expensive when compared directly to competitor offerings and prices. The laboratory inherently knew that its competitors did not offer such a full service, nor were they close in terms of the higher-than-industry-standards and care that the laboratory provided.

*The increasingly difficult position in which they found themselves, was having to continuously justify their higher fees to their clients and prospects.* They thought their fees should be sufficiently high to cover the perceived costs-per-sample, as defined by the age-old means of allocating a cost to each individual sample, based on an average of the overheads and operating costs associated with the business, allocated to each sample. They then added sufficient margin.

Their capital and operational costs were indeed disproportionately higher than those incurred by their competitors – for two reasons. The first is that they had a huge and excellent new laboratory facility and their finance people from the parent organization demanded that the capital costs of this facility would have to be recouped as quickly as possible, and the contribution from each sample would therefore have to be accordingly high. The second reason was that their competitors were by and large not what one would call 'blue chip': a basic service simply analyzing a sample and reporting on its contents could be done at a relatively cheap price as long as the client could tolerate an arguably sub-standard service that did not attract litigation or a significant compromise to their operations and obligations. The laboratory, in contrast, provided a premium service.

That left the laboratory in a quandary; *they looked too expensive for something considered as a commodity that could be purchased cheaper elsewhere.* The fact was that the client who required analysis of their samples only ever saw the laboratory as a 'stress' purchase – ie if they didn't need to buy their service other than to meet legislative requirements or to avoid some costly commercial risk (or worse, find themselves in court!), then they simply would not buy it at all. Period. They did not see any upside in purchasing the service and resented it each time they did. Therefore, when they had to buy such a service, they would simply try to opt for the cheapest supplier and quote that seemed to fit the basic requirement for a test result that met minimum standards and allowed them to make decisions and lessen some risk.

This problem instigated a real soul-search by the laboratory's management; 'how could we work up a good case to justify our high prices?' True, in terms of market positioning and perceptions they did have a higher price, but surely what the client actually received in return was much more than basic analysis; they surely got the best advice money could buy. They additionally received some 'free' consultation thrown in, and indeed a laboratory representative would occasionally act as an expert witness when called upon by a client. That and much more was given in terms of timely, confidential, informed and intelligent follow-up specialist advice, right down to helping the client with their own internal processes to find answers to many problems that surfaced during the ongoing analyses and improved understanding of client operations as the relationship developed.

'Not one customer was prepared to pay for the higher-than-industry price, and furthermore all purchases were considered a cost and a stress purchase.'

*Surely, they could just map out and communicate this 'extended product' and that was all that would be required?* 'Could we not just add this all up and ensure that the clients knew what they were actually receiving – even if they did not readily appreciate it or grasp the importance of dealing with us, instead of using a lesser service?'

It was soon determined though, that simply justifying all this 'added value' was still insufficient; everyone knew – including the clients indeed – that the laboratory actually did offer quite a bit more. They did appreciate that extra mile. They were actually quite complimentary when prompted to comment on the service when they had previously used it. *Importantly though, no one wanted to pay very much for it. Not one customer would wish to pay the 'margin' demanded by the finance people from the laboratory's parent organization, and each and every sample purchased was a real cost to the client – even, indeed, if that cost could be offset somewhat by charging other organizations further down the line.* So it was therefore an obvious case of the less money spent on samples, the better.

An assessment was made of the laboratory's situation in terms of its competitiveness. What lay at the heart of the problem was that the industry itself was not sufficiently differentiated right across the market – and when laboratories in the market did attempt to make some distinction, the market unsurprisingly didn't see anything apart from the difference in their pricing policies.

Any claims about USPs and differences didn't actually matter after all. Each and every client wanted to spend as little money as possible. Every sample was a cost, and if you consider something a stress purchase you grudge every single penny or cent you are forced to reluctantly spend. The client could see no benefit in spending more than they needed to or taking more samples, as each sample cost.

*The laboratory of course had a vested interest in selling and processing as many samples as possible; the more samples they received and analyzed, the more income for the laboratory.*

However, the more samples the client had to take, the more costly it was for them, with no assurance that the results would favour them any more than if they took the minimum number of samples or sent them to a different laboratory. *The clients wanted fewer samples to be taken and analyzed, the laboratory wanted more.* So everything was a negative for the client in this matter: probable costs they did not want, and the risk was high if they did not spend the money on samples or took too few of them.

**Therein lay both the core problem and the basis of a massive opportunity.**

The number of samples taken by the client company had no correlation to the value that either party would enjoy as an outcome of the engagement between the two organizations. The price charged for the analysis service didn't reflect the value either. It did reflect the unit/cost-plus pricing policy of the laboratory on one side, and the limitations on the number of samples that could be afforded and budgeted for by the client on the other. *If one party wanted to process more samples (the laboratory) and the other wanted to do less sampling (the client) then it became clear that we were facing a major and very apparent CONFLICT.*

This conflict was exacerbated by the fact that the client had to do a risk-investment calculation at every turn: did they risk taking as *few samples as possible* to keep their costs DOWN and afford appropriate sampling levels for all their projects (and perhaps overlook a major problem that might have arisen in the material they are sampling, and risk legal and commercial problems later) or did they take *as many samples as possible* to mitigate any problems and identify them earlier or more thoroughly, with correspondingly higher costs but perhaps little subsequent improvement to project delivery. The sublime and elegant solution lay in breaking the conflict between the 'many v few' sample options. What lay at the heart of the conflict was an underlying core problem that was identified and in turn resolved by changing to the client's currency.

*The issue?* (No one saw this coming.) The underlying problem for the *whole industry* was the fact that *ALL* laboratories *charged 'per-sample'*. There is insufficient room in this book to elaborate as to how and why this was determined, but it was irrefutable. An 'industry-rooted policy' – charging on a per-sample basis – led to the above conflict with the *resulting certainty that no one realized the true value of any relationship*. Both sides focused on price, cost, margins, numbers of samples and posturing, and not on real value to each party. That was partly due to the determination of 'value' as determined and calculated by the parent organization's finance people and the fact that the client didn't see much 'value' in a stress purchase that did little than just cost them money.

'Higher pricing and a fuller service didn't result in the client achieving any more objectives and didn't improve their project delivery.'

So the problem for the entire industry, and specifically for the laboratory and its clients, was that every laboratory supplier in their industry charged on a per-sample basis. But what was the alternative?

It may be easy for you and I to think that it would be simple to change to some way of pricing other than on a per-sample basis. That is easily said; think about this: your entire industry charges, expects and pays one way – all quotes, transactions etc are all done in exactly the same manner – do you think it would be easy for anyone to even *see* the need to change an 'industry norm', or that changing it could or would possibly give them an advantage? Would anyone wish *to change a rooted policy*?

We fought – and fought hard. We fought against the 'norms' of the industry, against the finance people who saw everything as cost-plus and 'contribution' per-sample. Incremental charging, unit costs and pricing, spreading costs and profit margin across samples – this was always the way and would continue to be. Correspondingly, securing sales of more and more samples was always going to be the target for the laboratory. The client base was similarly used to paying per-sample and making their daily risk–cost assessments. They indeed budgeted for that. But of course, the price and how it came about bore no relation to the value to the client, nor indeed did the client care how the laboratory or the industry came up with their prices and offers. The prices and practices just existed.

So, would it not just be a case of calculating and banding suitable sample frequencies and number crunching to produce a standard fee? That was hard; the undeniable logic was there – but as with many business issues, especially where there is an unarticulated and unresolved conflict, no one could see what and how to progress on that front. *Indeed, everyone was consciously now fighting the logic staring them in their faces.*

*'If you didn't move from a per-sample charging regime, you inadvertently COMMODITIZED your service and were destined to always be "on the back foot", competing against lower price alternatives, that were still on the same playing field as you.'* This mantra had to be absorbed and policies challenged. Something had to change so that the proposition was not the same as the rest of the market; this meant changing the pricing model.

Changing in the hardest of circumstances – to take a chance and do something that would be entirely alien, to an entire industry. *Yet change they did.*

Whilst fiercely fighting the norms of the industry that seemed indelible in the psyche of both the laboratory technicians and the internal financial people, we took the seed of a notion of charging other than on a per-sample basis and tested it with some clients. They liked it, but understandably wondered how it would work out in practice, whether it would be profitable for the laboratory and whether it was just a trick to tie them in to some long-term contract that in all likelihood would cost more than the minimum sample equivalent that may otherwise have been the case.

But like it they did, in principle. So we took it back internally and tested it with laboratory staff; we even included the reluctant financial people. The lab staff loved it; it offered them simplicity and saved them a lot of time (including a lot of time wrapped up in an unprofitable quotation process that was employed to work out how much an individual sample would be charged for each client, even if it was for one sample!). It allowed the staff to see that what they provided could be made more valuable and less of a stress purchase to their clients. It would be a lot easier to sell too. Instead of having to justify a high price, they could now offer a simple and attractive proposition. But did this mean it would make them more money?

*The finance people however didn't actually dislike it; they JUST DIDNT GET IT.* It went against the very nature and essence of cost-plus accountancy and, dare I say it, they even expressed distrust of their own client base that the client would perhaps abuse any – as they saw it – open-ended packaged deal. Finance thought not only that contract-based sampling could be unprofitable, but that the client would abuse the offer. Really? Clients who fundamentally do not wish to sample, and do not see themselves materially benefiting from sampling, would take more? (Indeed, it always cost them more than money spent on each sample, with additional time and processing and other costs on top.) Would they really want to get the laboratory to do more and more samples, overloading the laboratory and making it all unprofitable, just because they could under some new deal?

So, we asked the finance people: 'How many more cheques would they have to write out, how much more money would they have to spend if a client put in a few more samples per time-period than normal?' The result we got back? Not much more money, not much more in the way of costs. Indeed, very often there were no extra costs at all. 'But only if the client didn't abuse the deal'! So with one stroke, we turned the finance people around – for now.

I cannot say that we had them on our side forever – or since – but for that moment, sense and logic prevailed. But was this enough to break the conflict? Was this sufficient to make a breakthrough? After all, the clients did not want to pay much, or indeed anything, as they did not see much more than what could be construed to be just another selling tactic by a laboratory that wanted to make more money.

Therein lay the even more interesting opportunity – *the realization that the client also wanted to make more money.* The clients did not wish just to reduce their operating costs, which in this case were the costs of sampling and associated activities. They wanted to reduce their *risk*, 'flameproof' themselves both as individuals and as an organization, and indeed wanted to make more money too. Sampling was a cost and a loss, or at best something to prevent further loss. But they did not consider it to be gaining them anything substantive.

What I have not told you is that the initial companies we worked with – the laboratory's clients – were in the business of remediating contaminated land or 'brown field' land previously used by industry...

*'What used to be decisions all about costs and risks became an exciting discussion about rewards, partnership and making money.'*

'Brown-field' sites may be heavily contaminated with substances that have either an environmental or a human impact, or both. These land remediation companies had a real need: to project-manage the testing, treatment, removal of soil and underlying strata and generally rehabilitating an area of land, making it habitable or fit for re-purpose. Easy. That was the clincher. *The more land the client manages to remediate, the more money they make. THAT IS THEIR CURRENCY. The laboratory's currency – and that of all of their competitors – is NUMBER OF SAMPLES.* It was not rocket science – it never should be, such an elegant and practical realization – but it did make a lot of sense.

This meant that as long as the laboratory charged on a per-sample basis, then it would be seen as being the same as the rest of the laboratories out there. Working solely to its own advantage. Even seen as parasites perhaps – making more money by encouraging and demanding more samples be taken and processed. Each and every land remediation project was a risk and the client never knew the full picture or extent of the project they undertook at the outset. The more work they had to do to make the land habitable, the more it cost them. The land remediation client company's currency was at odds with that of the laboratory. You know intuitively what had to come next.

*The laboratory changed its currency to that of its client.*

The laboratory calculated how much effort would be required if it did not charge per-sample, if there were any operational hurdles to offering their client a firm and predictable (for the client) investment.

They worked out that the client, working flat-out, would need no more than an average of a given number of samples per time-period, even with the associated advice and service that may be required on top of that.

'You may not think that you have the means to change to a customer currency. Your competitor will not understand it. By all accounts and pressures you will be told you must be wrong. But the customer and the revenue confirm to you that you are right.'

So then the laboratory made them an *offer they 'couldn't refuse'*: no matter how many samples sent, the charge over the period of the contract would remain unchanged. The pay-off to the finance people was an obvious caveat that if the contract proved too difficult in terms of underestimating the amount of work, then the contract would be renegotiated upwards over time. The laboratory worked out how much would be achieved if the client could shift earth and contaminated land, and how much the client would need to invest in proportion, in supportive laboratory services.

The result was that the laboratory won two major contracts very quickly, each amounting to annual six-figure deals, and indeed expenditure for the clients on both deals was surprisingly greater than the sum of the historic transactions over the same period from the very same clients. We had started this particular journey trying to justify the laboratory charging what was perceived to be a high-cost service; yet we surprisingly managed to *GAIN MORE INCOME from the same clients* who were ironically initially under continuous pressure to spend less on laboratory services. They didn't see it that way of course – they now saw the service not as a cost, but as a means to make more money. This was not any kind of negotiating ruse or selling technique, but is a useful and clear example of a true and marked progress to move from margin myopia and constantly tweaking with differentiation, to changing to the client's currency. The laboratory more than satisfied a need; they became critical and close partners working without conflict.

So in summary, what was the change? The move over to the clients' currency meant that:

*THE MORE LAND THE CLIENT WAS ABLE TO TREAT AND MAKE HABITABLE OR 'REPURPOSABLE', THE MORE MONEY BOTH PARTIES MADE.*

Win–win. No conflict. They were both on the same side and working to the very same objective. There were no more discussions about how many samples and gambling constantly to offset risk. They both simply dealt with the rewards. That was very satisfactory. Hundreds of thousands of pounds sterling worth of 'satisfaction' for the laboratory and millions of pounds worth of satisfaction for the clients. The laboratory's fundamental change wasn't to do with what they provided – it was to do with how they provided it through recognizing and reacting better and *more fully* to their client's need. Its obvious, yet unarticulated and unseen need: to shift more land.

The laboratory? No longer seen as selling samples, but a *true partner improving the ability to shift dirt.*

The competition? *They were left wondering what the hell happened...*

**FIGURE 9.2**   Chapter 9 summary action table

| ☑ | CHAPTER 9 Summary Action Table |
|---|---|
| ☐ | Determine what 'rooted' policies exist in your marketplace and within your organization that may be preventing you gaining more revenue |
| ☐ | Check for bottlenecks in our delivery process; any constraints that cause problems for the customer down the supply chain; can we help remove or reduce those constraints? |
| ☐ | Challenge yourself with the idea that you can 'more from margin' to something more worthwhile<br>  – Test pricing policies v value<br>  – Review how your customers make money<br>  – What is preventing them from making more? |
| ☐ | Create an indelible, sustainable process that allows you to constantly sense needs by focusing on uncovering the customer currency and acts as a distinctive win-win |

© Copyright David James Hood: Competitive SME

**FIGURE 9.3**    Summary of the essentials from this chapter

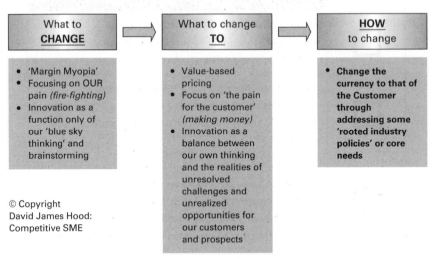

| What to **CHANGE** | What to change **TO** | **HOW** to change |
|---|---|---|
| • 'Margin Myopia' <br> • Focusing on OUR pain *(fire-fighting)* <br> • Innovation as a function only of our 'blue sky thinking' and brainstorming | • Value-based pricing <br> • Focus on 'the pain for the customer' *(making money)* <br> • Innovation as a balance between our own thinking and the realities of unresolved challenges and unrealized opportunities for our customers and prospects | • Change the currency to that of the Customer through addressing some 'rooted industry policies' or core needs |

© Copyright
David James Hood:
Competitive SME

> *The most important single central fact about a free market is that no exchange takes place unless both parties benefit.*

**MILTON FRIEDMAN**

# Grasping the opportunity 2 (SALES)

## 'Changing to managing the INCOME (revenue) PIPELINE'

> *If you want to make God laugh, tell him about your plans.* **WOODY ALLEN**

**P**rice, price, price, price. Arguably, the most difficult of the 'Ps' of the marketing mix to set, manage, optimize and maintain. But more importantly, this is the marketing component of our business on which we all seem to fixate when it comes to sales and selling, almost to the exclusion of any other issues to do with the market.

We make the mistake of supposing – or at least allowing ourselves to be duped into thinking – that income and revenue strategies are the same as the related issues to do with pricing: we try to set prices as a corollary of value, yet we are constantly under pressure to lower prices, and indeed low prices are mistakenly seen to be the same as 'cost effective' or 'less expensive'. We think that 'lower pricing' somehow equates with greater value, will make the product or service easier to sell, and that all would be improved if we could just offer more unit sales for a lower price. Likewise, it is not merely about 'lowest' or 'total' cost of ownership for the buyer or any resulting cost reductions or cost avoidance; these are simply purchasing benefits and not powerful operating benefits for the customer to improve their competitiveness or well-being.

The previous chapter outlined the need for an aspiring SME to move to a more relevant and profitable focus and financial measurement whilst steering clear of margin myopia: to effectively change to *value pricing based on the customer's currency*. This chapter sets out a complementary course for the SME to better develop and measure sales as a process and activity, so that SMEs get the most out of this important aspect of their business, which matches the drive towards a real change to exploiting the focus on the customers' currency. It also makes it easier for the SME to set realistic, achievable sales (revenue) goals.

The aim here is to stand traditional sales thinking on its head: to use the new Competitive SME competitive marketing way described in this book in sensing and responding to the market and thus helping the SME to make better sales management decisions and to improve and sustain its sales pipelines more effectively.

Tendering – going for the lower price – is unlikely to be the best way of constructing good proposals. Look for opportunities to go and see your customers, sense their needs outside the immediate tender requirements and add on real value – which may actually cost less than you think. *Indeed 'lowest cost' to the buyer does not mean best value, despite what we may assume.*

Buyers rarely just want a lower price; they need a job done further down the chain and this needs to be uncovered deftly by changing the currency from bartering, trade-offs and margins and adopting a fresh and principled new approach to sales management and operations. The customer does not want lowest price; he or she wishes major competitive improvement and to maintain or increase income and profit.

##  Reconstructing the sale

In remembering that value is its own real number, and is not the result of setting a very subjective numerical 'price point', we can eloquently start to deconstruct our offer and reconstruct it with true value related directly to customers' needs. Use the simple illustration shown in Figure 10.1 in conjunction with the 'total product concept' outlined in Chapter 7.

> SME\ *'Improving your chance of a sale is not all about providing cost reductions or avoidance for your prospect or customer.'*

**FIGURE 10.1**    De/reconstructing the sale

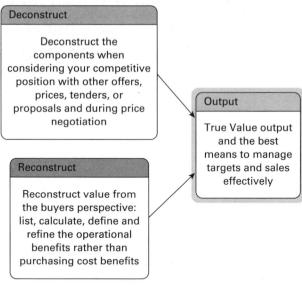

© Copyright David James Hood: Competitive SME

The fantastic example shown in the previous chapter of 'changing to the customers' currency' and grasping the opportunity to enhance marketing, effectively demonstrates this 'deconstruction' process. It of course was not just a proposition or a product; indeed the actual 'product' traditionally described as 'sample analysis' was nothing to do with the actual value of the offer. This meant, in sales terms, that the core product had been suitably deconstructed to examine what the customer actually got, what the supplier actually could do, and most importantly, what constraints were placed on the customer's competitiveness and money-making capabilities by their circumstance that might be reduced or removed by the supplier. Then it was reconstructed as a superb win–win deal.

Therefore, as the above illustration suggests, sales activities may not only be more productive, but would be better served by moving to a means of sales target setting and management that reflected the elegant and powerful change to the customer's currency. The laboratory in the example didn't see its targets as cumulative sales of individual samples any more – that was simply a measure, not of value but of incremental units of income to them – but changed it to setting and managing income based on a share of the money they made for the customer. In turn, this was of course easier to sell! The salespeople loved it too.

# Move from anticipating loosely-predicted targets based on sales transactions to focusing on 'a crafted pull from the market'

In addition to using the worthwhile 'which means that...' test when considering 'features and benefits' to crystallize what they really mean to your customer or consumer, try and further translate those benefits into real money-making for your customer and major numerical value for your market.

The manager or executive responsible for sales can work with marketing and sales to move beyond discussions about features and benefits to start to set a price that reflects true value rather than margins, illogical cost-plus calculations or some other spurious calculations that have nothing to do with the market. *If you are selling to a business customer, it is worthwhile having a policy and mind-set that reflects the fact that people do not buy to spend money; they buy to invest that money.*

One of the best ways to reinvigorate your negotiating and deal-making when it comes to selling is dealing with price issues and objections before they happen – right at the outset. As negotiations progress from initial discussions right through to proposals or tenders, pricing is usually a thorny issue that is traditionally left till the selling organization gets through its lists of features and benefits and then 'sells' to the customer. That is why discussions concerning 'price' usually follow lengthy statements, presentations etc, as no one really wants to talk about it earlier and the selling organization wishes to have a chance to talk up the proposition before handing the downside to the would-be customer – what it will actually cost them.

Traditionally, price is not left to the end in error; it is usually left to the latter part of any sales engagement to ensure the salespeople have had time to pile in as many features and benefits and 'reduced the reluctance to buy' before hitting the customer with a 'cost'. If we were comfortable with our price as an *investment* – we would not leave this to the end, would we? We wouldn't try to hide it away, but would ensure that the customer saw the value in their investment from the outset. And we would be happy to share the expected returns.

If you deal with pricing early, in the way that is described in this book, then the prospect or customer sees value and a sound investment and not a 'cost'. Dealing with any 'objections' early – although the word 'objections' could be said to mask the real issue – means grasping an early opportunity not only to indelibly work up your difference in terms of features and benefits but to change everything to the customer's currency and demonstrate that you are *confident* in what you are charging for those benefits.

*Customers prefer sellers who are direct and honest, do not skirt around issues and who are clear and confident about how they are placed competitively in the market, especially when the USP is evidently based upon their specific needs.* That is the best way to deal with 'objections' – don't give yourself or your customer cause to see pricing as 'objectionable' from the outset.

 It is a great place to be if you can confidently say to the prospect or customer:

I can categorically state that my price may not be the lowest; my price will reflect an honest proportion of the real value I help you create. I would love to have you as a loyal customer and return that loyalty and this can only be achieved properly if I unearth your true needs and build value that helps you directly sustain income or make more money, or resolves some important problem for you. Please let me demonstrate how we compare, where the value we think we can create actually is, what it is and how we can work together on income improvement and reducing your costs in other areas apart from price, and let you see a clear and marked return for your investment in us.

It is sometimes very difficult to get out of the price trap as a selling organization. Consider though, when you are making your own purchases and looking at your options for products, services and suppliers or the possibility that you may wish to switch suppliers and perhaps the type of products or services. *You know very well that it is not just about the price when YOU make a purchase.*

You know that when you even start to look at possible options to change your own supplier, there are painful choices and changes to be made: processes, resources and product or services that may have to be modified, strategies upset (and a few people likewise) and a whole host of problems and difficulties arise – even if you know that to change your supplier or product would attract a lower price (commonly known as switching costs). You would be making a change to ensure that some strategic or operational issue was resolved; you would be looking for gain – further income – or reducing risk or a 'hurt' – fear of loss. Furthermore, you buy using a process that involves making investment decisions.

 *As a business purchaser or as a consumer yourself, you do not buy just on price alone, so it is an advantage to remember this when dealing with your customer too.*

Also, remember that many of your customers – or prospects – are looking to switch or buy from you as opposed to another source as they may be currently dissatisfied in some way. (Or indeed, they may simply be underperforming and blaming suppliers and others rightly or wrongly for their lack of income.) Of course, many of your customers or prospects may be 'happy' with their current supplier, yet even here the techniques described in these final chapters can help you make the switch that much easier for them.

*There is a good chance that their current supplier hasn't unearthed, clarified and defined precisely why their own customers buy and what actual value that current relationship has.* This is your opportunity to revisit, clarify and refine what they need, and one that enables you to demonstrate to them your true understanding of their business and its needs. This is one of these times when an SME can really shine – it can understand its customer's or prospect's needs just as much as any larger corporate – and very often much better and with greater rewards in securing long-term contracts.

When comparing and working up your value proposition and dealing with price for your customer or prospect, you can use a simple formula similar to the one suggested in Figure 10.2. The equation shown there offers another exciting and interesting opportunity; you can address the middle component 'downside' by negating it somewhat. In addition to the benefits, translated into financial figures in the 'Full value' component, you can then look at reducing the downside with the prospect or customer – which actually opens up the opportunity for adding more benefits and real value to the proposition specifically for the customer. This makes sense, but you can be assured that your competition isn't taking this structured approach to helping the prospect or customer reduce the downside or 'risk'; *all your competitors will be doing is trying to justify their price. You are doing something quite different – you are demonstrating your VALUE.*

**FIGURE 10.2**    Determining value v price in the eyes of the prospect or customer

| The Net Value to the Prospect or Customer of your Proposition | **=** | Full Value (as determined by your sensing activity and 'change of currency' with your prospect or customer) |

**minus**

Downside (eg switching costs, necessary change, 'perceptions of problems')

**minus**

Price that you are charging them for your proposition

© Copyright David James Hood: Competitive SME

Of course, you can tie in your initial full value determination with a test or pilot of your product or service and, if you have conducted your sensing and value proposition development properly, the customer would be willing to try your offer. They will very likely wish to work with you subsequently if there are any risk elements later while or after the tests are conducted, as you have willingly demonstrated your integrity and capability from the outset. The 'downside' part of the equation also gives you an opportunity to give the test or pilot trial of your product clearer decision criteria from the outset; this means that if the customer is testing your proposition along with others, you are the one in the driving seat when it comes to the test criteria, by offering and agreeing the criteria up front.

By helping your customer effectively test yourself, you again are demonstrating a great deal of integrity and transparency. You are making it clear that if you do not gain the value for them, you don't expect the sale from them. You are now managing the pace of the opportunity and increasing the chance of pulling in an earlier sale by creating a new sense of urgency and priority for the project.

The above equation allows you to construct not only the price *with* the customer, it helps you articulate to them how you have constructed your offer and at the same time, powerfully demonstrate what the difference is between the price they will pay for it and what it gains for them. And of course, how much of a welcome gap there is between the two!

 *'There is little point in wasting effort in trying to justify your price when you should spend precious time demonstrating your value.'*

ADDITIONALLY, if all of this wasn't sufficient argument for you to change how you develop your proposition when in price competition with others, by adopting a real value approach and mitigating risk *you are helping your prospect or customer – the individual or individuals involved in the buying decision – to SHINE.* By coupling their investment decisions with a new focus on their currency, you are giving them a genuine means to deliver return on investment, which is something that they need internally, and which they constantly have to prove and improve. If you are helping them with that burden too, then you make yourself a true and important partner indeed.

*You have helped them help themselves.* They may even be seen as a centre for excellence and remarkable at 'driving a bargain' for their organization and making profitable change. You know however, that they didn't get a 'bargain' – they got true value and both parties shared an even-handed amount. A lot better than self-defeating arguments over margins, justifying two separate negotiating positions or wrangling over price, don't you think?

Oh, and always remind the customer, once they are buying, just how much you are saving and making them! (By checking and sensing, using WOM management, and mitigating any more risks and negatives for them whenever you can.)

# Changing sales targeting and management

When setting sales targets, planning activities and sales operations, we usually carve those 'projections' from annual into quarterly and monthly figures. We break them down for good reason: we need to ensure a consistent pipeline of sales and smooth delivery on orders over the course of our financial periods. The way companies have done this has not changed for a *very* long time; each and every SME more or less will look at chopping up the annual targets to ensure that they are delivered in equal chunks and cash flow maintained accordingly.

As these measurements – and figures – are arbitrary and may be errone-ous, can or should we change the way we conduct the sales process and measurements to something that perhaps would result in more meaningful and precise sales efforts? We know that our efforts to come up with the annual, quarterly and monthly sales targets and resulting individual incre-mental sales figures are purely guesswork. We know that they are rarely accurate. We know that in setting targets we are only looking at what we wish for or hope to achieve; these figures are based on data that by its nature is historical and unlikely to be repeated. But we have used these ways for so long, and so do most businesses. We would do well to reflect on the following: if we have explored an 'outwards-in' perspective and appreciated that changing to the customers' currency is a good thing for our business, then what exactly is our currency? If we are changing to the customers' currency, and going to deliver not on 'unit sale' but with a focus on an irrefusable offer based on value, then why the need to have targets set and implemented in the same way we have always done?

*Unit sales are not the currency of the customer, nor should it be ours. What then, should be the focus for sales?*

Changing your annual total sales figures to the front end of the year and putting a buffer at the end is a fantastic way to rid the SME of the stress and demoralizing and counterproductive emphasis on monthly or quarterly sales figures. You could use the buffer as a percentage of annual sales and then get down to managing the real sales income rather than arbitrary monthly or quarterly figures.

A new buffer-management style of sales (and marketing) approach could smooth out sales management and order fulfilment for production; this helps everyone operationally and lessens the need for 'panic production', with the resulting greater consistency for call-offs, batches etc right through to delivery. This would also have a mirrored positive effect on your purchasing and ordering efficiencies and effectiveness (and your inventory levels if you have stocks). This could, if effectively implemented, lead to taking the pressure away from selling units to move us towards selling value. We do not have the space here to explore fully the concept of sales management by buffer rather than by repeating quarterly and monthly figures, but let us think about this notion for a minute or two. We all know that the sales process throughout any given year is patchy, is somewhat cyclical or chaotic, is interfered with by forces outwith our control (and indeed by simple issues such as vacations for our people and our customers).

Yet we strangely assume that every quarter or monthly period will involve precisely the same activity and face the same issues, and we expect each to deliver the same income. Each month or quarter end makes us do strange things, including offering promotions and deals at the end of the period, just to make some arbitrary deadline date! These time periods actually determine what we do, how we sell, what activities we do when selling, and all without any hint of a concern for a customer need. Needs come and go; customers want to speak to us when they want to, not when we want to; our targets regrettably become the ongoing focus rather than great delivery of our proposition, or ongoing understanding of our markets.

*Indeed, the way we measure is at the heart of the problem of misalignment between our marketing and our sales efforts.*
Let us look at the following statements; they don't make sense and it behoves us to change to a system of sales targets and management that makes a lot more sense:

- Yearly sales targets are usually cut into discrete, equal quarters.

- Apart from assuming all time periods are equal, this results in some illogical behaviour by all involved in sales and management.

- For example, salespeople may 'coast' when targets for the quarter are reached – a natural human reaction.

- Conversely, when their figures are not being met, bad decisions and actions are undertaken by them and their management that affects the business, purely to 'make the figures'.

- Salespeople want low unit targets; the board and management want high unit targets.

- Salespeople want targets based on facts, that challenge them in a positive way; owners and senior management want figures based on their desires and expectations.

- Salespeople get good rewards (presumably) when sales come in early (ie in any quarter or month, they exceed target); *yet* if they do better in one period, they are still expected to get the same or more in the next. The salesperson has little impetus or desire to over-deliver. Or indeed to bring in sales in a way that fits with either marketing campaigns or production capability.

- Marketing campaigns rarely chime with the similarly constant changes in sales effort and results; likewise little marketing or sales activity chimes with the ability of the organization to actually deliver to those expectations.

- Marketing activities can delay sales operations and can be completely out of synchronization with each other.

So... what about a adopting a system that:

- Encourages salespeople – and channel partners – to pull in sales 'early', yet doesn't penalize them for not meeting every monthly or quarterly target.

- Is based of course on real-time market sensing (this has been covered earlier).

- Means that management, marketing and sales all focus on the monthly target (rather than quarterly), ensuring that the sales function achieves these figures (and exceeds them) and where necessary picks up any under-target sales and prevents ingress into the buffer.

- Any addition to the buffer (time and resources saved up) can of course be used for more sales activity, but it also allows the option to release some prime time with the customer, doing further needs analysis (constraints and identification of further needs) or time to develop increasingly favourable word of mouth and resolve customer service issues.

- *The only target is the annual INCOME target rather than spuriously construed quarterly sales and we ONLY MANAGE THE BUFFER.* Rather than 'flogging' our salespeople and channel sales partners, we concentrate on building our buffer resource. Altogether much more productive and beneficial!

Using buffer management in the sales process means a commitment to the following, with resulting benefits to both personal stress and income generation capability:

- Keep the figures as income revenue, not units or items.

- Start by using a figure from your enquiry/order pipeline that is always outstanding and add it to the yearly target (eg last year's turnover was say 2 million; all things being equal, it could be 2m again, but at any time you may have 300,000 in quotations and proposals 'out there' that you consider very likely to happen. This could be real money, remaining uncollected from the customer at any one time, or not acquired by you.)

- Place two to three times this 'outstanding' figure as a *buffer* on to your previous year's revenue figure.
- Place one-twelfth of the buffer figure for each month as a target.
- Load them into your spreadsheet or other system; using the above example (for illustrative purposes only):
  - 2 million (your own currency);
  - 300,000 in cash could be 'out there' at any time;
  - two times this figure is 600,000 as a buffer;
  - 1/12th of the 2 million, plus 1/12th of the 300,000 = approximately 192k per month; lets call it 200k per month for simplicity (Table 10.1 gives these in units of 10,000).

**TABLE 10.1**  Determination of price buffer management

| J | F | M | A | M | J | J | A | S | O | N | D | **Buffer** |
|---|---|---|---|---|---|---|---|---|---|---|---|---|
| 20 | 20 | 20 | 20 | 20 | 20 | 20 | 20 | 20 | 20 | 20 | 20 | **60** |

Therefore, Table 10.1 shows that in this example the sales and marketing people and functions have monthly revenue of 20k rather than quarterly target. It is suitably ambitious (being greater than last year's equivalent, with the addition of 'always out there' possible revenue) and offers the 'comfort' of having a buffer that can both make up for shortfalls (eg due to cycles) and *that becomes the main and common measurement for all involved with revenue generation.* The buffer amounts to a value equivalent of three months' target revenue and should prove sufficient; if this drops well below 60, proportionate action needs to be taken and if it exceeds 60, then extra income is coming in and/or more time can be spent identifying and developing the changing needs of the customer and market. This system encourages all to bring in the money now, rather than later; traditional quarterly measurements of course, do not encourage early sales. Oh, and the buffer could be a *rolling* figure, so none of the myopic 'this year' terminology as it is always a rolling buffer – and we can leave 'yearly figures' to historical accounts and necessary financial returns as required by law!

Buffer management, and the associated management of sales and marketing, will be informed and guided by the WOM feedback from your market. Good WOM will help improve sales and subsequent recommendations, and help to increase the buffer accordingly. Albeit unrefined, buffer measurement and supporting the buffer can provide a powerful new metric common to both sales and marketing.

- Make it clear to your salespeople and agents what you are doing; you are front loading your year and creating an ongoing buffer figure;

also explain that you expect all to focus on income rather than unit-sales generation (unit sales will look after themselves!).

- *Ensure that marketing is loading likewise; if sales figures slip badly in any particular month and the buffer is severely affected, marketing and sales activity increases; if income is surpassed then the buffer is unaffected and capacity (including your salespeople) is released to offer more help and support to the customer.*

- Salespeople and the sales process do not fixate on monthly targets any more; the salespeople and others understand that the objective is to maximize income, not meet permanent unit-sale targets.

- Marketing and sales work together to make money rather than fight over differing cycles, events and activities; all work with, measure and manage the one buffer figure; *they both work to PROTECT THE ONGOING BUFFER.*

- Get buy-in from all; ensure that they understand you are moving to a real-time revenue-generating model from an arbitrary and historical unit-sale model.

- *Reward the sales effort for NOT BITING INTO THE BUFFER rather than for meeting monthly targets.*

*'Sales and marketing people and managers can now keep a constant eye on sales constraints (in terms of time to pull in cash from an enquiry).'*

Besides, if all goes according to plan, think what the above will do for your organization's agility! Your customers should be happier too, as they will see more transparent policies, less pushy and stressful sales efforts, and improved delivery of product and service at a number of levels. They may even get to see your people when you are not trying to sell them something! If you can reduce stress and inappropriate targeting methods and associated activities from sales, and give them the means to offer an 'unrefusable offer' as in the laboratory example – imagine the sales revenue that could be achieved!

Good sales-buffer management is the beginning of a fruitful and virtuous cycle with positive knock-on effects in production, quality control, stock control, finished goods, supply chain management, reduced delivery times and, yes, *it could even offer a firm opportunity to actually INCREASE your price in the supply chain.*

Imagine feeding direct market and customer input, secured through managed word of mouth, into your improved sales quota-setting and revenue management activities that also can positively affect production and operations! The ability to sense-and-respond and achieve ongoing adaptability and resilience would at last, be truly achievable – and 'built in to the fabric' of your SME.

## Changing the way we look at sales

In moving from annual projected unit-sale targets that manifest as quarterly and monthly 'milestones', to realistic, real-time and buffer-managed sales, *we progress from the traditional process outlined in Figure 10.3 to the one shown in Figure 10.4.*

**FIGURE 10.3**   Changing the way we look at sales (1)

© Copyright David James Hood: Competitive SME

**FIGURE 10.4**   Changing the way we look at sales (2)

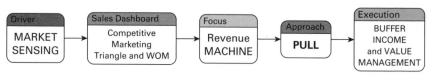

© Copyright David James Hood: Competitive SME

Figures 10.5 and 10.6 show the overall change in emphasis and benefits to the SME in grasping the opportunities made available if you can make this fundamental change to the way you manage sales. The first shows the current situation for most SMEs and the second the opportunity to make the change to a new currency. This new way ties in well with our stated objective of 'making to order' rather than making to sell, as the following demonstrates.

## *Current process: finding sales*

Figure 10.5 illustrates the link between our current behaviour and policies that result in increased and perpetual stress for the individuals and the

**FIGURE 10.5**    Current v new sales process (1)

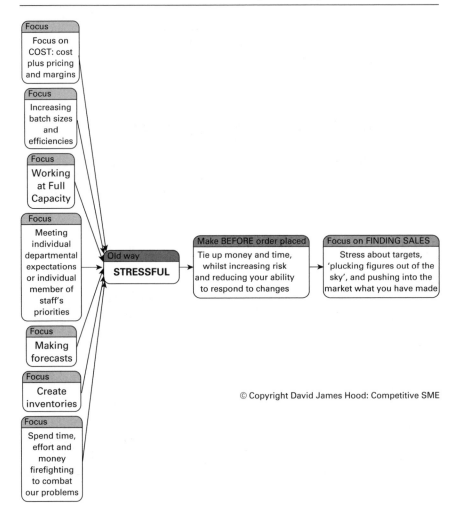

© Copyright David James Hood: Competitive SME

whole SME, as it frustratingly strives to meet arbitrary figures. We make to sell and have to find someone to sell to; 'selling to' becomes the objective rather than satisfying and maximizing income and well-being for both the SME and the customer.

## New process: managing revenue

Figure 10.6 shows the necessary conditions to drive agility that are underpinned by the new process of coupling WOM-led projections and value-add practices and activities with buffered sales management. The result? An ability to change to 'make-to-order' and an approach that your customers

**FIGURE 10.6**   Current v new sales process (2)

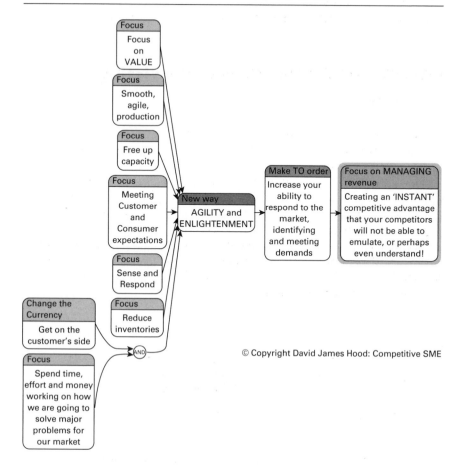

© Copyright David James Hood: Competitive SME

will find a whole lot more persuasive and interesting than your focus on sales targets!

## Convinced yet?

What is comprehensively, yet simply, recommended in this book is a lot more than just 'playing with words and numbers'; what you can achieve is changing a 'major rooted policy' that all SMEs and others have concerning sales management – *sales management could and should act in REAL TIME*.

In 'taking the heat off' striving for unit targets in a given period and transferring that 'heat' to working up new propositions based on your customers currency, then it is win–win. If you pull your sales 'targets' – or income requirements shall we now say – earlier in the year, then you can free up some valuable resources to make even more money for the customer and improve their lives. You could even give some of that away 'free'. The customer will subsequently not just see the SME when it has something to sell to meet its incremental targets – they will see this new approach as genuinely acting to help them make more money as a true partner should.

# Improve post-sale service to existing customers

It is an ongoing problem – and therefore an opportunity for the SME owner or manager reading this book – that most organizations constantly focus on seeking out and acquiring new custom.

The old saying that it is more expensive by a factor of five to seven (or more) to find and sell to new customers than to sell to existing customers, is attention grabbing. This declaration, whilst true, omits to highlight an important accompanying point: that it is consequently easier to constantly *engage* with your existing market and its customers (and be *engaging*) rather than try and hook new custom continuously and having to develop from scratch that same degree of trust, confidence, brand and evidenced delivery that your existing market values.

'A great way to break the pendulum that is having excess stock or stock shortages is to better understand the market and use a buffered system of sales management.'

Simply put, SMEs do not have legions of salespeople or agents to look to secure new business and attract new customers; they have a finite and usu-ally very small sales resource. That precious resource should be applied to the market that the SME has already invested in rather than simply trying to invest in new, spurious markets to improve income. This is not to suggest that the SME should not seek out new markets; it is just stating the simple fact that we should not overlook the very – and best so far – markets and relationships in which we have invested a lot of time and effort (and indeed that our customers have invested in also!).

'Suppliers frequently mistake high volume customers as key accounts'.

(Beth Rogers)

*A side-effect of wrongful focus on the constant quest for new customers leads to attrition of our existing customer base.* A customer base that values us, and which we should value in turn, is constantly shrinking as the customer goes elsewhere whilst we turn our attentions to other markets and prospects rather than serving them! And, we have the audacity to think that they are disloyal when they decide to go elsewhere!

# SME  Stop thinking about sales as 'units of delivery' or transactions

The fantastic example shown in the previous chapter demonstrates an effective strategy to change to the customer's currency. It reduces and removes our predisposition to thinking about sales – and pricing – as simple arbitrary transactional units of measurement that do not in any way reflect true value – value neither for you or your customer. We need to think beyond so-called 'lifetime value' of a customer as just a combination of transaction figures and how often those transactions are made. *Transaction metrics do not reflect value, profitability,* and mask your best options for *advanced competitiveness.*

Historical transaction information, is just that – *historical.* It is to do with occurrences that probably will never happen in the same way again; people change, companies change, markets change, needs change. You change. What matters is not how often people buy and how much they spend; *what matters is the scale of the change affected by you in the customer or consumer's lives.* You need to have that approach if your organization is really to change from providing minimal purchasing benefits to significant operational benefits to the market; we need to get away from seeing customer or consumer 'churn' as just something to manage by en-suring you find more customers or consumers to replace those that you have lost. An examination of numbers based around historical transactions and 'ticket prices' leads us to overlook new opportunities, fuller needs satisfaction and competitive challenges, and *stops us using more appro-priate measurements.*

The future is non-linear, so your sales graphs based on historical projec-tions will not be realized!

*A small increase in customer RETENTION can lead to a multiple pay-back in increased profits*; not just in maintaining the income from those customers, but through leverage that gets you much more than if you were to replace them with others. This goes for both a business customer and a domestic consumer; keeping them makes you more money than finding them, and keeping them means they ask others to come along too. If we can free up more time and resource to focus on sincere customer retention, the consequential ROI can be proportionately massive.

Good sales buffer management can free up time for retention activities and ensures that the SME has a more consistent and constant level of engagement with the market.

If customers or consumers change in terms of their needs and wants – which will happen of course – and if you consider them to be more than 'transactions and ticket-price', then you will see those changing needs and wants more clearly and readily. You will be able to re-categorize their profile on an ongoing basis and perhaps see their needs and wants long before your competitors do. Only when we break free of the 'transaction trap' will we truly be able to grasp the opportunity outlined in the latter chapters of this book and make the MOST money out of the relationship with the customer or consumer.

You need a process and policy for sales that you can have faith in, and a worthwhile proposition that you can believe in likewise. Then the customer or consumer will start to believe also...

**FIGURE 10.7**    Chapter 10 summary action table

| ☑ | CHAPTER 10 Summary Action Table |
|---|---|
| ☐ | Deconstruct the price of your existing and/or new proposition |
| ☐ | Reconstruct it in a way that makes sense and gives you and the Sales people or agents confidence to sell |
| ☐ | Construct a new, simple, buffer based Sales Management system; use trigger buffer levels (low = action, high = capacity freed to do more for the customer) |
| ☐ | Set up a meeting with Sales and Sales Agents / Partners to present and get buy-in to the new sales target-setting and management method |
| ☐ | Keep reminding all people that it is a ROLLING system, so that everyone is focused, always, on the goal of revenue generation, at all times |
| ☐ | Present the final system to all involved in sales and marketing, channel partners and customer services. Compare it with the 'old way' and outline the benefits of the new way |
| ☐ | Check and realign the time we spend on attracting new customers v serving the existing customers |
| ☐ | **Understand and test how a new WOM system combines with buffer sales management acts as both a barometer of our potential in the market and the effectiveness of our marketing campaigning and sales activities** |
| ☐ | Constantly measure the buffer and use buffer management and target-setting as a rolling figure and reflect this approach in your scheduled meetings and planning |
| | © Copyright David James Hood: Competitive SME |

**FIGURE 10.8**    Summary of the essentials from this chapter

| What to **CHANGE** | What to change **TO** | **HOW** to change |
|---|---|---|
| • Misalignment between marketing and sales; between financial targets and market realities and dynamics<br>• Having to 'justify our price'<br>• Low sales agility | • A sales process that maximizes sales activities and time spent in pursuit of the goal to make money<br>• Confidently demonstrating value<br>• Proactive sales activities and process | • Change sales from an aggregate of transactions to one of maximizing value<br>• Release time for salespeople to serve<br>• Change the way we see targets and manage sales income figures<br>• A rounded, confident pricing process is in place that incorporates the simple 'determining value' step **with** the customer and providing a real shield against commoditizing your product and helping you articulate your differentiation<br>• **Use a BUFFER MANAGED sales process that compliments marketing activity** |

© Copyright
David James Hood: Competitive SME

*I have never worked a day in my life without selling. If I believe in something, I sell it, and I sell it hard.* ESTÉE LAUDER

# Quick wins (rather than quick fixes)

## 11

*Efficiency is concerned with doing things right.*
*Effectiveness is doing the right things.* **PETER DRUCKER**

This section summarizes what you can do quickly to make the change to marked new competitiveness and marketing capabilities. What to change, what to change to and how to change.

## Change 1: What you think of marketing and its role as the means to competitiveness

Look to gain maximum buy-in from your colleagues (once you have convinced yourself to move forward as described in this book!). Think of marketing more in terms of 'reducing time-to-market, propelling an enhanced and optimized proposition into a more targeted and willing marketplace'. To find and turn market needs into that market wanting to engage and buy from you. If any change does not result in delivering a decisive competitive advantage, then it is not a real change for the better. And one cannot have a decisive change that does not involve the market and its needs. Invention is just that, without innovation – the means to make money from our technical capabilities and creations.

## Change 2: Sensing your market

Customer surveys must be transformed from just a marketing research tool into the basis for a practical scoring system, then fed into an operating system to sense and respond to the market. Your new WOM system – a real 'customer relationship management' tool – is a key driver in sensing 'what I should do and whether I am doing it correctly and delivering real value'.

# Change 3: Less of an obsession with our competition

We have assessed the time, effort and resources we employ in checking and fretting about our competition; we have looked at their proposition using our marketing tools and compared them to ours. The 'gap' has been identified, developed and evidenced; we have translated that into our 'marketing mix' and – using a change to customer currency – made our proposition truly unique and ultra-competitive.

We have asked ourselves 'are our "competitors" or those in the market we consider "competition" truly such?' Or do we simply *think* we are wooing the same prospects and customers, using similar 'industry-type' messages and descriptions of 'what we do'? That is neither a definition of competition nor indeed of a competitor.

# Change 4: Review what success means and our strategy to achieve it

Realize that success is not incumbent on being the largest seller in the market, or having some dominant sway over it; it is about you meeting the needs of your market better than others – and having your customers tell everyone else about you. Unbeatable profit and well-being for you and your customer or consumer is the goal; it is not to make and sell as many 'units' as possible. So try to change your thinking, internally within your SME, as to what success actually means to you and your colleagues and how you will measure it:

- 'I have identified major constraints that prevent my customers (or consumers) enjoying the financial or other rewards that they should be experiencing.'

- 'I have been able to create an evidence-led proposition that is valued by them and meets their needs better than other propositions in the market; I agree to develop, measure and adopt value propositions based on the market's perception of their value.'

- *'I have started out on the road to try and achieve remarkable WOM ranking; we are now on a path to sense and respond the market and to constantly test and improve that process.'*

- *'I have started to indelibly change how we view sales as an income-generation rather than a unit-sale process through using buffer-led target-setting and management.'*

- *Market leadership is now defined by how well we do the above as we have DEFINED OUR OWN MARKET!*

SME *'We only have a very narrow definition of customer need: that which we can identify only in terms of a description of our product!'*

Couple these all together, in time, to grasp and secure the virtuous new marketing and sales tenets of changing to the customer's currency, removing a focus on margins and pricing squabbles, and changing to an income/revenue buffered sales management process.

Don't think your customer, consumer or prospects are simply complacent or that they lack suitable understanding or knowledge about your product or service so that is why they are not biting your hand off or overly concerned with what you consider exciting and worthwhile.

The likelihood is that they have more burning and priority problems elsewhere to attend to, or may have greater or more apparent opportunities that are similarly pressing on their own precious time and finite resources; or either your or your competitors' propositions may simply not be meeting a real need in a profoundly effective way, or mitigating their perceived (real) risks associated with spending time and money even just considering your offer.

When exploring a proposition with a prospective or existing customer, we often assume that they have unlimited funds or resources to invest (we know that they don't, but we act and sell as if all spending decisions were simple if the prospect could only could be persuaded). We usually have only a very narrow definition of customer need: that which we can only identify in terms of a description of our product.

We need to show that our proposition does not just 'fit the bill', but it is something more profound than other suppliers' offerings. It solves real problems and would be more worthy of their precious investment than substitute 'improvements' to their business. Remember, your SME is not just up against other SMEs for the opportunity to sell and supply a product or service they offer; you are always up against other investments that your customer or prospect could do with their money. There is constantly some substitute on offer; there is always another fire to fight or opportunity in which the customer can invest. We can ignore that reality time and again when we get hypnotized by the transaction, price and persuasive selling processes.

# Always ask for testimonials

One of the best ways to ensure your competitive advantage is to identify it and help nourish it in your customers, so they develop a USP based on your actions.

Grab everything you can that is to do with your sphere of influence; you should have all your strands of branding elements and simple things like your domain and online markets identified, targeted and secured. All these elements are intellectual assets too – the knowledge you have gained from your research, the contacts you have gained and nurture, the seemingly disparate elements and communications around your proposition and what you provide (including domain names and how you interact online with your markets) all add up to not just a potent mix in product or proposition terms, but are real 'money in the bank', intellectual assets that can increase your competitiveness both now and in the future.

Remember, those intellectual assets are not just the usual, obvious manifestations of 'knowledge' that you may have within your SME, such as the technological advance or the patent that you have or provide; it can be the actual processes and how you deal with your market that can really make the difference. And that ultimately will determine whether you can create and maintain a resilient, agile organization.

# Cautioning about 'quick fixes'...

*Although there are quite a few tools and suggestions in this book, it makes sense before you even attempt to look for a 'quick fix' to attempt the short marketing audit from Chapter 2.*

This will perhaps give you an impetus to follow through and use more of the tools and policies presented in these pages. One of the best ways to become competitive, to enhance your proposition and to ready your organization to identify and exploit 'quick wins', is to address the problem of 'marketing myopia' expressed as the conflict explored earlier; *lets tackle our unending focus on margin to the detriment of value.*

**FIGURE 11.1** Current v new sales process (1)

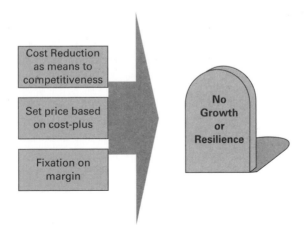

**FIGURE 11.2** Current v new sales process (2)

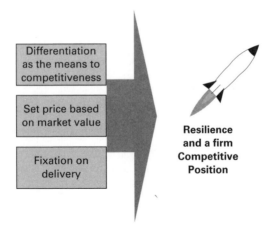

# Tackling your immediate concerns and improving now

Of course, you may wish to 'cut to the chase' and deal with some burning competitive issue now, before making and enacting a proper marketing plan. That is the real world!

Apart from cautioning against moving forward without recourse to good analysis and the construction of an excellent new plan, you can of course use the marketing tools listed in the following table to quickly assess your competitive situation. The 'action table' in Figure 11.3 gives you some tools and ideas.

# FIGURE 11.3  Tool action table

**Quick Action table**
(examples of challenges and recommended tools to use are for *illustrative purposes only*; use of the tools should be based on your own SME's challenge and situation!)

| SME Competitiveness Issue or Requirement | Marketing Audit | SWOT | Proposition Accelerator Tool (PAT) | Market Research & Word of Mouth | Write the story / Comm's loop | Product Life Cycle | Perceptual Mapping & Planning | Brand Management cycle | Segment Market | Reconstruct the Sale | Testing the Proposition | Change to the Customer's Currency | Change to a Revenue Pipeline | The Extended 'Product' | Value Proposition / Matrix | Competitive Marketing Triangle | Marketing Mix check |
|---|---|---|---|---|---|---|---|---|---|---|---|---|---|---|---|---|---|
| Branding & Positioning | ✓ | ✓ | ✓ | ✓ | ✓ | ✓ | ✓ | ✓ | ✓ | ✓ | ✓ | | | ✓ | ✓ | | ✓ |
| Refining the Proposition | ✓ | ✓ | ✓ | ✓ | ✓ | ✓ | ✓ | ✓ | ✓ | ✓ | ✓ | ✓ | | ✓ | ✓ | | ✓ |
| Pricing issues (driving down) | | | ✓ | ✓ | ✓ | ✓ | ✓ | | ✓ | ✓ | ✓ | ✓ | | ✓ | ✓ | | ✓ |
| Product issues (tired product) | ✓ | ✓ | ✓ | ✓ | ✓ | ✓ | ✓ | ✓ | ✓ | ✓ | ✓ | ✓ | | ✓ | ✓ | | ✓ |
| Market issues (shrinking market) | ✓ | ✓ | ✓ | ✓ | | ✓ | ✓ | ✓ | ✓ | ✓ | ✓ | ✓ | ✓ | ✓ | ✓ | | ✓ |
| Poor contact with market | ✓ | ✓ | | ✓ | ✓ | | | | ✓ | | | | ✓ | ✓ | | | ✓ |
| Major competitors squeezing me | ✓ | ✓ | ✓ | ✓ | ✓ | ✓ | ✓ | ✓ | ✓ | ✓ | | ✓ | ✓ | | ✓ | | ✓ |
| Need to diversify | | ✓ | ✓ | ✓ | ✓ | ✓ | ✓ | | ✓ | | ✓ | ✓ | | ✓ | ✓ | | ✓ |
| Costs overall are too high | | ✓ | | ✓ | | ✓ | ✓ | | ✓ | ✓ | ✓ | ✓ | ✓ | ✓ | | | |
| Lengthening product development times | | | | ✓ | | ✓ | | | | | ✓ | ✓ | | ✓ | ✓ | | |
| How do I invest in marketing? | ✓ | ✓ | ✓ | ✓ | ✓ | ✓ | ✓ | ✓ | ✓ | | ✓ | ✓ | ✓ | ✓ | ✓ | ✓ | |
| I don't have a marketing resource | ✓ | | ✓ | ✓ | ✓ | | | | | | | ✓ | | | ✓ | ✓ | ✓ |
| I don't know where to start | ✓ | ✓ | ✓ | ✓ | ✓ | ✓ | ✓ | ✓ | ✓ | | | | | | | ✓ | |
| Margins are becoming tighter | ✓ | ✓ | | ✓ | ✓ | ✓ | ✓ | ✓ | ✓ | ✓ | ✓ | ✓ | ✓ | ✓ | ✓ | | ✓ |
| Increasing customer demands | ✓ | ✓ | ✓ | ✓ | ✓ | ✓ | ✓ | ✓ | ✓ | | | ✓ | ✓ | ✓ | | | ✓ |

If you do choose – wisely – to do the fuller assessment and planning activities outlined in this book, I would like you to continue to develop your plan and carry out the sequence for competitive advantage using the following tools, which are explained in Chapter 12:

- the business and marketing planning cycle;
- the competitive marketing dashboard.

Figure 11.4 summarizes some immediate options to action and offers some examples of some of the burning issues that an SME is contending with at any time.

**FIGURE 11.4**    Summary of the essentials from this chapter

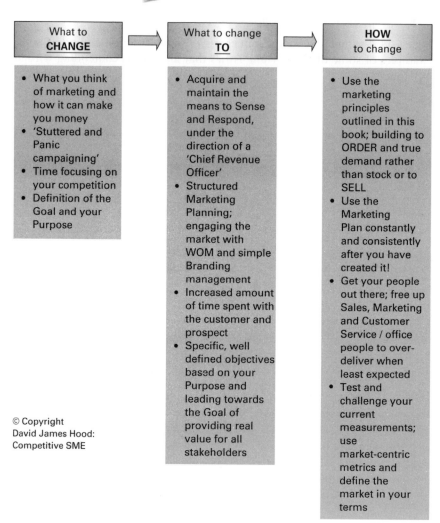

competitive SME™

| What to CHANGE | What to change TO | HOW to change |
|---|---|---|
| • What you think of marketing and how it can make you money<br>• 'Stuttered and Panic campaigning'<br>• Time focusing on your competition<br>• Definition of the Goal and your Purpose | • Acquire and maintain the means to Sense and Respond, under the direction of a 'Chief Revenue Officer'<br>• Structured Marketing Planning; engaging the market with WOM and simple Branding management<br>• Increased amount of time spent with the customer and prospect<br>• Specific, well defined objectives based on your Purpose and leading towards the Goal of providing real value for all stakeholders | • Use the marketing principles outlined in this book; building to ORDER and true demand rather than stock or to SELL<br>• Use the Marketing Plan constantly and consistently after you have created it!<br>• Get your people out there; free up Sales, Marketing and Customer Service / office people to over-deliver when least expected<br>• Test and challenge your current measurements; use market-centric metrics and define the market in your terms |

© Copyright
David James Hood:
Competitive SME

> *Most ailing organizations have developed a functional blindness to their own defects. They are not suffering because they cannot resolve their problems but because they cannot see their problems.* **JOHN GARDINER**

# Optimizing your proposition and making more money

## 12

## Bringing it all together!

> *All human development, no matter what form it takes, must be outside the rules; otherwise we would never have anything new.* **CHARLES KETTERING**

## A cyclical planning process for the SME

Figure 12.1 presents a summary of the use of enhanced, direct and practical marketing as the definitive means to possess competitive advantage for the SME. Using the tenets shown in this book, managed through your marketing planning process, leads to consistent management of income by maintaining and growing your competitive edge. Marketing is, and can be, more than 'just promotion' and offers a means to compose and collate all your business activities 'around the customer' and hence develop and deliver real value.

## SME The competitive marketing triangle

Managing and optimizing the triangle is a great means to focus all your marketing and revenue-generating efforts on the income pipeline. The triangle not only demonstrates what needs to be done at any

**FIGURE 12.1**    New SME business and marketing planning cycle

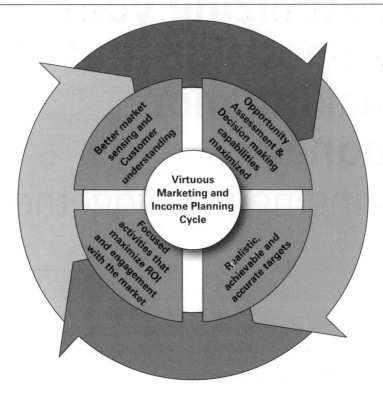

Better market sensing and Customer understanding

Opportunity Assessment & Decision making capabilities maximized

Virtuous Marketing and Income Planning Cycle

Focused activities that maximize ROI and engagement with the market

Realistic, achievable and accurate targets

© Copyright David James Hood: Competitive SME

time, but it allows the SME manager or executive to focus on the three most important issues affecting the three major measurements that concern everyone: *money now, money soon and money in the future.*

It is simply not good enough to fill the pipeline with 'might buy' prospects and throw money at promoting to them. Shouting – telling, yelling and selling – again, is simply not good enough. As SMEs aspiring to become more profitable and productive, we need to ensure that word of mouth is captured, maintained and optimized, and in such a way as to improve our chances of gaining money now, soon and in the future.

What is needed for the SME is a dashboard that ensures management tackles one of the major problems for small business – cash flow – whilst keeping an eye on the market, its opportunities, and of course bringing in future revenue. The competitive marketing triangle acts as the prime measurement of how the company is faring in terms of revenue, and how it is maintaining its competitiveness through this book's tenets of adopting a firm

**FIGURE 12.2** Competitive marketing triangle

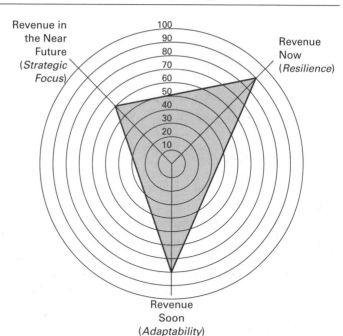

© Copyright David James Hood: Competitive SME

strategic focus, resilience and adaptability. The triangle is laid out as a radar graph in Figure 12.2, and the metric is identified as evidenced revenue. This requires some critical work on your part to set in place some meaningful calibration and metric for these axes, but at least with an eye on those axes you can ensure that money will come in now, soon and in the near future.

## Using the competitive marketing triangle as the strategic dashboard for your organization

You can use your competitive marketing triangle to reflect the sales figures from your new sales buffer management process.

*'How often have you heard someone say "The company I dealt with surprised me with something valuable that they didn't have to, but chose to do so"... Probably never.'*

### Revenue NOW

- maintaining and improving *resilience*;
- engaging with the market;
- improving communications and channels;
- figures can be taken from your current *MONTHLY* sales revenue performance (cash, not units or transactions);
- value on the radar map = new buffer managed monthly sales target.

### Revenue SOON

- becoming adept and *adaptable*;
- building and maintaining a WOM marketing system that leads your proposition changes and improvements (see the following pages);
- your current and pending marketing activities and campaigning should be maintaining your overall *BUFFER* – the status of your overall buffer is stated and managed here, showing if you are being successful (maintaining or growing your buffer) or lagging in sales (biting into your buffer);
- value on the radar map = buffer level (0–100; 50 = nominal buffer).

### Revenue in the NEAR FUTURE

- securing a real strength in having a *strategic* focus;
- alignment of your creativity with market reality;
- adopting a strong, disciplined approach to what changes should be made in the organization, cutting down change to where it matters most;
- at all times, adopting a 'customer currency' assessment of major supply chain and partner opportunities when creating proposals;
- figures can be taken from your efforts to evaluate your market and creating and evaluating your existing and constantly changing and sharpened propositions to match the *customers' currency*;
- value on the radar map = money identified based on the customer currency in the new pipeline.

## Proposal development

Key items checklist for creating a business-to-business proposal:

- Check how your proposal creation process aligns (or not!) with customer sensing.

- Hot spot issues for the specific customer (check 'Roots for reception' in Chapter 4).
- Change to their currency.
- How you are partnering them.
- What extras are included that are: a) essential; b) form part of your evidenced USP; and c) don't cost too much.
- Guarantees.
- Look at the customer-facing and delivery skills you have now and those that you will need (incidentally, too much CPD activity – continuous professional development and in-company training – is focused on operational expectations rather than customer or proposition-specific skills related to income generation; see how your customers can 'train' your people to deliver to them better!).
- Make sure that it reads and is communicated as an irrefusable offer.
- Remember at all times that you are dealing with humans – an individual person or group of people – rather than just a cold blooded, logical 'corporate dispassionate entity'; living, breathing human beings with a need to be helped, engaged with and offered a really good (and proven) reason for buying.

Radar-map key components and look at vocational UK Marketing & Sales Standards for skills that may link with proposal development.

 *'The objective of any company is to implement an effective and lasting process of ongoing improvement.'*

*Just as the main summary sections of this book focuses on 'what to change', 'what to change to' and 'how to change' your proposal ought to similarly follow this format;* not only to work up the whole proposition, but so that you and your people all buy into, and understand, what the proposition and proposal actually is and so that the customer is absolutely clear what they will be receiving and why it is better than anything that they may be offered elsewhere:

- the major customer needs that have to be addressed (what to change);
- what the proposition is (what to change to; a refinement of those needs and the breakthrough offer);

- what you will deliver (how to change; how it will be achieved);
- the 'currency change' and how you will charge based on that currency;
- *... so that it all MAKES IT EASY FOR YOUR PROSPECT or CUSTOMER TO SEE 'WHAT IS IN IT' FOR THEM.*

# SME\ Improving communication

The idea of 'positioning' your proposition in the consumer or customer's mind has been covered earlier in this book, but it is worth reiterating that we need to better grasp this and behave in a way that is congruent with real positioning. By that, I mean we should always be aware that positioning is not about simply creating messages and ploys that seek to coerce or trick the recipient into believing that our proposition is somehow related to some wonderful status.

It is about hard and fast realities and that we can only really improve our own positioning within the market if we take positioning and our related communications with the market seriously, and base everything on the identification and resolution of real needs and wants.

That is not to say that we should not be creative in our messages, our communication with the market. We should indeed be creative and innovative; but remember, there is a disparity between trying to be different and making a real difference in the minds of those you would wish to have as consumers or customers. You have to edit – to cut down any copious correspondence and written 'copy' into 'silver bullets' that strike at the main hot spots for your market. They would care to 'hear the sizzle, rather than the bacon frying' but they also need to know 'why the sizzle is good for them'.

Remembering why people are attentive to certain key elements and not others is important in refining your communications and making them more effective; the measurement of effectiveness is whether you have succeeded in causing some action in line with your objective. Some observations about improving communications:

- Make sure it '*sings*'; it must make the recipients sit up, take notice and ring true with them (in that it must be recognized as something that is currently a concern to them).

- People look to buy something that prevents, reduces or stops a problem (fear of loss), or helps them achieve or acquire something (want for gain); *what does your proposition do for them?*

- It must *paint a picture*; you have seen logos, slogans and other pieces of 'communication' from organizations that do not convey anything meaningful. If any piece of communication needs to be explained or translated, then it is very unlikely that it will readily hit the mark, much less result in an action. It has to be seen through the 'so what?' prism to check it makes sense.

- *All your communications should be congruent and fit with your overall positioning strategy*; remember you are maintaining and growing your brand; it must fit with other pieces of communication and value that you have previously used and will use in the future; no piece of communication or activity is in isolation from the others.

- You have to know not only what people or organizations want, you have to *know what motivates them.* This should affect your strategy when refining and improving your communications; likewise, you need to check what form of communication the prospect, customer or consumer prefers to use, and what the different motivational factors are for different individuals and groups. Segmentation based on need is badly requiring an overhaul for SMEs, but an added dimension is further segmentation based on motivational issues and variances; tying in both of these issues means your campaign will be more effective and you will waste less money on unnecessary or unwarranted campaigns.

- *It is not just about giving value; it is about the recipient feeling valued.* It is insufficient to simply state what value is on offer; you have to make it crystal clear that the recipients, when they do something or even just receive your messages, are sincerely and demonstrably important to you and your organization. Try to get them to IMMERSE themselves; this means in addition to telling them their input/response/purchase/opinion/action etc is important, you *reward them* afterwards and make it clear that they are valued. And reward them often.

- Encourage (and ask, where appropriate) them to *pass the message on.* This is ultra-important in good word of mouth marketing (for obvious reasons) and in this new digital age is something that your prospect, customer or consumer can do readily, sometimes in less than a few seconds. If you don't ask for the 'viral' message to be passed on, it probably won't be handed on or transmitted.

- *Ask for and use testimonials post-sale and grasp the opportunity to initiate real customer service with the customer at that time*; make sure that this is built in to any sales (and after-sales) process and a reminder set up to frequently remind you and your people to ask for testimonials. They are golden. Those responsible for customer and consumer service after-sales should check that the buyer is using the product or service you have supplied to best effect. Make sure that they are, and your ongoing contact is more advanced and engaging rather than just entering into a conversation that starts with 'I am just calling to check if there are any problems' – as this is negative. Best to use openers and state your intent using positive introductions and opening statements such as 'I know that you have purchased x recently, and I am calling to ensure that you are happy with the product and the delivery process, and to see if there is anything you would like to chat about regarding our service overall. Indeed, I would like to invite you to be on our customer panel if you would wish to; this only means feeding back some thoughts now and then to help us help you and our other customers. We actively engage with our customers after the sale has been made, and to keep you as happy as possible and (enjoying the product/making more money) on an ongoing basis'... and give them a reward if they join the panel. The more complex the product, the more dimensions there can be to customer service, after-sales engagement and rewards.

- *Check any refinements*, when and where you can, with some of your target audience to whom your message is targeted. This sounds difficult, but a simple telephone call to a good customer to ask them 'what they think of this latest piece of information' may be all it takes; they will tell you, and you can change or refine your communications as necessary; they know much better than you if it will work or not.

- Sign off: at the end of your communication, whether it is an e-mail or a short advert, a web page or a leaflet, your sign off has to do two things: *ask for action and put across the definitive USP.* Your last – and lasting – impression that the recipient needs to be left with, is the position that you would wish to have in their conscious and unconscious minds, that they need to do something (and there is sincere, obvious and real value in them doing so) and that they continue to 'enjoy' receiving your messages and engaging.

- *Remember, at all times you are communicating WITH the recipient, not TO the recipient*; your intention is to engage with them, which then inspires them to follow up with an action, not to interrupt them with trivial and irritating statements; write or construct messages as if you were creating the most important and elegant poetry or short story!

# Lastly, and most importantly – how to measure word of mouth and optimize it

Simply put, one of the best ways to manage and maximize word of mouth is using some form of 'net promoter score'. Essentially, one looks to examine the market, and gauge the likelihood of any customer or consumer (or prospect) recommending a company, product or service. In our rampant desire to group complex business tools and measurement models, we overlook the simplest and most profound means of maximizing our brand, proposition and position in the market. You may of course, be somewhat sceptical that word of mouth is something that can be managed or indeed maximized. What we need to do here though, is demonstrate what it actually means to measure, manage and actively increase positive word of mouth.

'Essentially, word-of-mouth marketing is all about finding out and maximizing how much of your market – potential and existing customers – would recommend your proposition to other buyers.'

The following gives a ready example and foundation to manage WOM:

- It is all about increasing the proportion of your engaged market who 'would gladly recommend' your company, product or service proposition – this is the main metric for WOM. They have to be asked that direct question for this to work; and asked 'even if you chose to currently buy from elsewhere'. You can also couple that question with one that asks: 'Did we meet with your expectations that you had prior to the sale?' if that applies.

- This means that the market – or more correctly the part of the market that you currently or previously were in contact with – must be asked whether they would recommend you to others.

- Once this is established, you plot out those people who would recommend wholeheartedly, on a scale right down to those that may never recommend or indeed may be 'hostile' due to some incident or are negative through poor perceptions of your product, proposition, company or an individual personality issue.

- As simple as this sounds, it is far from simplistic and does need a degree of discipline to establish consistency in conducting frequent and meaningful measurement of the efficacy of your WOM sensing and responding system; consistency and constancy are the key doctrines. It can only really work when you keep to a formula and use a system that the market, and those within it who become engaged with your WOM activity, understand and appreciate.

- We are working on advanced – but simple – WOM and proposition-accelerating tools and the reader is directed to the Resources section in this book and register their interest in receiving updates on these subjects as they progress.

Whatever questions you use to supplement the 'are you likely to recommend?', they should not be open-ended if possible, unless it is specifically to do with the market's emerging and as yet uncovered needs. When using any type of marketing or market research activity that uses 'Likert' scales, make sure that they are constructed only with an *even number of options*; this is a major failing in research (you will see that most are odd numbered).

Odd numbers can lead to a disproportionate number of middling '3s' or '5s' – ie people not making any kind of decision or taking the middle road. That is no use to you; you need to encourage them to make a judgement, even if it is made without due information, knowledge or considered opinion, as perceptions can be uncovered using an even-numbered, forced-scale approach.

An example of a WOM metric is given in Figure 12.3. The figure serves as an example only; it is thoroughly worthwhile to take some time and work out your own with an appropriate scale, wording and system to inform and manage those measurements. Broadly, you do not wish too many different categories, as this becomes unmanageable and will result in time spent on concerns with fine detail and descriptions rather than getting the job done – the job of moving people from the 'left to the right' of the above scale, thereby seeking to increase the proportion of those favourable and more likely to recommend. A useful clarification as to what the individual categories are, that correspond to the above metric, is given in Table 12.1.

**FIGURE 12.3**    Example of a WOM metric

Remember, the boundaries between the above categories are blurred; we are dealing with behavioural and perceptional issues that will never be hard and fast and absolute, only relative. And of course, extremely subjective.

What is more important is that we create and keep to a standard means to measure and demonstrate both our willingness to listen and influence in a genuine way the perceptions of our brand in the market, and the market's subsequent receptiveness to our brand and our overall proposition.

It must never be used, or seen to be used, as simply a cynical ploy to manipulate, just an excuse to ask for recommendations and testimonials, or a ploy to be referred to an individual's personal colleague or contacts, or lead to any abuse of trust.

You can use e-mail to seek a response; indeed e-mail is a great way to perform WOM main scoring on a constant and consistent basis (but beware

**TABLE 12.1**   Word-of-mouth management

| Category | Description |
|---|---|
| **ADVOCATE** (warm and has or is likely to recommend) | • Has stated categorically, without too much promoting, that they are happy with the product and service of which they have first or second hand knowledge<br>• Would actively, or have actively recommended and provided a referral |
| **EFFECTUAL** (welcoming & receptive and could recommend) | • Have been more than passive prospects or customers and have indicated a willingness to occasionally engage with our SME<br>• Have provided a testimonial stating how favourable they are to your company, product, service or proposition |
| **FLOATING** (indifferent and unconcerned) | • May or may not have purchased in the past, and have shown little interest in becoming engaged with your organization<br>• Or show firm 'loyalty' to a competitor or otherwise do not see you as their solution to their needs |
| **WHOLLY DISINTERESTED or ANTAGONIST** (We have got a job to do) | • Have or have not purchased, and presently do not see you as uppermost in their minds to the point that they may not wish to hear from you<br>• May have had a real or imagined bad experience or perception, reinforced at some time, that makes the individual confrontational or more likely to bad-mouth and affect your position in the market |

of the usual caveats and dangers of soliciting feedback too often!). Likewise, any complementary or corresponding online surveys you may use to help with your research and WOM management should keep to the above rules.

There are far too many online surveys that are too lengthy, seem to be going nowhere, are blatantly one-sided and are offering nothing obvious in return for the respondents. *You must, wherever possible, give something substantive in return for their efforts and in giving you valuable knowledge.*

The same must be said for solicitation for WOM feedback and e-mail or online surveys. Give the customer a profoundly good reason to 'comply'. After all, they are not going to think much of your credibility if you are asking them about the likelihood that they will recommend you, if they think you appear to be taking them for granted. Feedback data is one of the most important items in business and the customer or consumer knows well that their information and knowledge has a value and they therefore need to feel valued in any exchange.

The best thing about this approach is that coupling WOM with a customer reference programme (a glorified way of saying that you are going to ensure you get your testimonials and that customers and consumers are actively encouraged to recommend you) can deliver an elegant approach, and one of the easiest and most cost-effective activities you could perform to improve your business – and it can be done quickly.

**FIGURE 12.4**    Summary of the essentials from this chapter

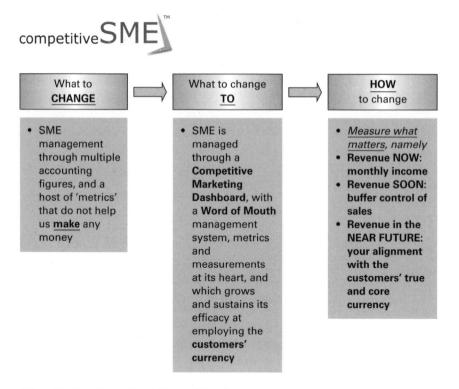

competitiveSME™

| What to **CHANGE** | ⟹ | What to change **TO** | ⟹ | **HOW** to change |
|---|---|---|---|---|
| • SME management through multiple accounting figures, and a host of 'metrics' that do not help us **make** any money | | • SME is managed through a **Competitive Marketing Dashboard**, with a **Word of Mouth** management system, metrics and measurements at its heart, and which grows and sustains its efficacy at employing the **customers' currency** | | • *Measure what matters*, namely<br>• **Revenue NOW: monthly income**<br>• **Revenue SOON: buffer control of sales**<br>• **Revenue in the NEAR FUTURE: your alignment with the customers' true and core currency** |

# The whole Competitive SME process

Figure 12.5 offers a staged plan to utilize the tools and inspirations presented in this book. It is difficult to prescribe a 'definitive way' to sequence these components although I have made an effort at the start of Chapter 1 to help you on your way; it is nevertheless worthwhile that you should undertake these tasks. To consider instead the virtues of value over cost, market pull rather than push, word of mouth over insincere promotions, ridding you of margin myopia, focused activity over a shotgun approach and by turning to the customers' currency and thereby creating and delivering real value WITH the customer rather than FROM them. I commend this approach to you and look forward to hearing about your efforts and, hopefully, your participation in the fuller futureSME programme.

Thanks for reading through this book and I wish you a mutually prosperous future for your SME, working in partnership with its customers and other stakeholders.

*David James Hood*
*The Competitive SME Project*

'We have to ensure, through careful sales buffer management coupled to our new marketing strategy and planning, that we free up sufficient time for those responsible for our sales and marketing activities to consistently identify constraints in the market (needs), manage and maximize word-of-mouth and fill our new revenue pipeline!'

**FIGURE 12.5** Competitive SME proposition enhancement and improved competitiveness through marketing

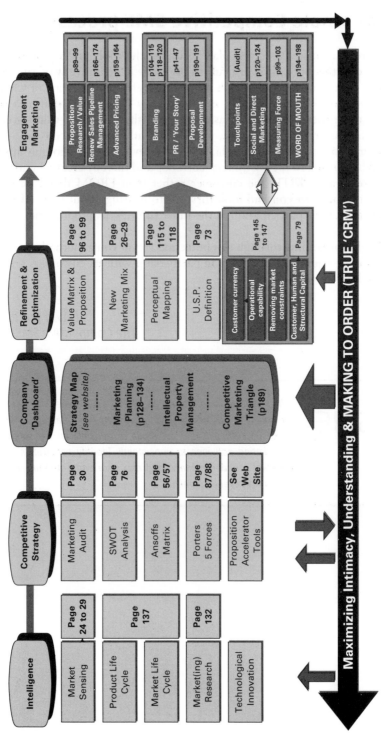

# RESOURCE APPENDICES

# MARKETING AUDIT CHECKLIST

**A** short summary marketing audit checklist is given below; it is a summary of earlier components featured in this book.

## Quick marketing audit

- How well do you know your immediate customer?
- How well do you know your end-user customer or consumer?
- Are your product and service improvements and any major changes based mainly on internal or market input?
- We have adopted a pricing policy that best reflects the market's needs and the customer-evidenced idea of value.
- Price confidence level: how confident are we that we have set the best price that reflects our value to the market?
- In terms of 'people-hours', how much time do our customer-facing staff spend proportionately between internal meetings and external conversations?
- How happy are you that your brand 'position' – what your market thinks about you – is well placed in the market?
- Like most organizations, we have options as to where and how to communicate and promote to our customers; do we only try a few, or as many as possible?
- We consistently and constantly review and update our publications – that is, all the brochures, websites, sales literature etc 'to try and keep our market up to date' with our messages and latest proposition announcements.
- We speak to our customers or consumers post-purchase and place them firmly within an after-sales plan (or schedule in at least a number of calls/contact opportunities to keep them informed and engaged).
- We use a feedback system or at least record any customer feedback that we receive *other than* using a production quality system (such as Six Sigma).

- We include our customers and prospects in our product improvement and *development* process on a structured basis.
- We follow up on all customer or consumer complaints with a resolution and ensure they are satisfied.
- Have we identified all people – internally and externally – that are involved in *any and all* customer-facing, 'value adding', contact with the product or customer and managed, trained and resourced them accordingly?
- Do we have a designated person or people for the role of marketing and ensuring 'constant and consistent contact' with the market?
- Where do we lie on the scale from reliability to response? Do we care more about quality processes and 'getting production of the product more efficient', or have a greater focus on responsiveness to customers and the market?
- How long has our recognized competitive advantage lasted in the market recently?

# FUTURESME

## What is futureSME?

FutureSME is a pan-European initiative with 26 partners including 13 small and medium-sized enterprises (SMEs), 10 R&D organizations and universities, two SME networks and a second-level school. The project partners are from the UK, Ireland, Sweden, Italy, Turkey, the Czech Republic, Poland and Slovakia.

The objective of the initiative is to develop a new practical business and manufacturing model for SMEs in Europe, which will enable them to compete successfully at a national, European and global level. Therefore, futureSME's vision is:

*'Igniting a movement across Europe and leading SMEs towards sustainable business models in order to transform SMEs into wealth creation machines for Europe.'*

## Who benefits?

FutureSME support tools and methods are primarily targeted towards manufacturing SMEs. The tools and content are developed in a simple and effective SME-friendly language. Also some of the audit tools, case studies and e-learning packages can be used by consultants, regional development agencies, advisors, practitioners, trainers and educators. Although futureSME is targeted for manufacturing SMEs, some of the frameworks, concepts, management tools and techniques can be equally applicable to larger companies from manufacturing and services as well as non-European SMEs.

## How does it work?

The future is uncertain and unpredictable therefore SMEs should continuously evolve, improve and adapt to the emerging environment to survive and sustainably grow. To achieve this, futureSME offers a four-step organizational transformation process called PATH (problem, assessment, tools and holistic growth).

**www.futuresme.eu**

# GLOBAL MARKETING NETWORK

## Global Marketing Network
When we talk marketing, we really mean business

Global Marketing Network is positioned as the worldwide professional body for marketing and business professionals. Over the past five years, GMN has built a growing network and achieved an enviable reputation and momentum for its vision, as a result of which GMN has:

- a global collaborative network of universities, business schools, membership associations, publishers, trade councils and business groups fast approaching one million people worldwide;
- a growing portfolio of strategic global partners providing leading-edge business support and professional development solutions;
- the commitment and enthusiastic support of a world-class Global Faculty comprising many of today's most widely respected and most-published marketing thought-leaders – who regularly work closely with many leading organizations and brands and whose textbooks are recognized as the leaders in their field;
- a Global Advisory Council and Country Advisory Councils featuring senior business professionals and leading marketing scholars, working together to help define and shape the future of the marketing profession.

After global consultation, Global Marketing Network has now implemented the world's first global accreditation system for the marketing profession, enabling marketers around the world to be rewarded and recognized for their professional achievements, against globally established standards. The first 1,000 professional members of Global Marketing Network will also receive a share in its success. To find out more about applying for

Professional Membership, or to become a Standard Member for FREE, please visit **http://tiny.cc/gmn-sme**.

Darrell Kofkin
Chief Executive
Global Marketing Network

# Microsoft

**http://crm.dynamics.com**

Microsoft, the world's largest software company, is placing itself and its sizable resources fully behind the marketer and marketing.

Its CRM Dynamics product has been evolving over recent years, to not only become a major customer relationship management tool, but to quickly and now effectively offer both a 'premises' and online version of the product and one that has some marked 'XRM' platform capabilities and extensions to the product to increase functionality and productivity for the marketer.

Through supporting this book, and further ongoing developments and consciously aligning itself with the marketer and marketing, Microsoft has stated its intention to be at the forefront of revenue-generation capabilities for its customers; helping marketers, managers and indeed anyone who is responsible for income-generating and customer-facing activities.

Author of *The marketing manifesto* David James Hood welcomed both Microsoft's support for the book and their aligning themselves with the marketing profession. Hood said 'It is great when such a major player in a sector looks to truly align itself with a community of practising professionals; in this case managers and marketers with a responsibility to bring in income for the organization. Microsoft is well known for making business software to help companies run more efficiently, now it seeks to additionally help businesses make money effectively.'

# PARTNERS AND RESOURCES

The Epsilon Project™ is an important new cause and ongoing initiative to develop and bring to the marketer and manager definitive and robust campaign management and new proposition optimization capabilities, optimizing and reducing the many variables of the marketing mix. Simply subscribe to the initiative to keep abreast of all developments as they happen. Simplify marketing; get products, services and campaigns right as early as possible. Reduce the noise. Make better decisions.

www.theepsilonproject.com
www.twitter.com/projectepsilon
The Marketing Manifesto™

# CORPORATE CONVERSATIONS

## David James Hood PgDIM PgDED PGMN

The author David James Hood is available for speaking engagements, internal workshops or 'corporate conversations' about enhanced competitiveness for your organization.

David is a Professional member (PGMN), a member of the advisory panel for GMN, and is also its CPD Director.

### David's online details

http://ie.linkedin.com/in/davidjameshood
(please feel free to link with me if you have bought the book!)
'Corporate Conversation' enquiries: **davidh@mymarketinglife.com**.

# ONLINE RESOURCES

**www.competitivesme.com**

**@competitivesme**

You can access a full range of supporting Competitive SME tools, methods, events and other valuable resources at the Competitive SME web site.

As a Reader, I value you and would encourage you to come to the web site, check it periodically, and of course sign up to any Twitter or other announcements.

I hope to meet you in person sometime, either at a 'Competitive SME' event!

David James Hood

# INDEX

*(italics* indicate figures or tables in the text)